SCIENCE FACTS

MIRACLE OF LIFE

Chameleons, like this Parson's chameleon from Madagascar, can
move their eyes independently of one another.

A pair of Southern elephant seals sparring in the water off the coast of Argentina. Males can grow to over 21ft (6.4m) in length, and weigh up to 8,000lb (3.63 tonnes).

SCIENCE FACTS

MIRACLE OF LIFE

LIONEL BENDER

CRESCENT BOOKS
NEW YORK • AVENEL, NEW JERSEY

CLB 2751

© 1992 Colour Library Books Ltd., Godalming, Surrey, England.

This 1992 edition published by Crescent Books,
distributed by Outlet Book Company, Inc.,
a Random House Company
40 Engelhard Avenue, Avenel, New Jersey 07001

Printed and bound in Italy

ISBN 0 517 06556 8

8 7 6 5 4 3 2 1

The Author
Lionel Bender is a writer and editor with nearly 20 years of experience of
producing illustrated information books for adults and children, mostly in the
fields of science and natural history. He has an honors degree in Biological
Sciences from Birmingham University, England, and is a Scientific Fellow of
the Zoological Society of London, and of the Linnean Society. He has
written more than 35 books himself, and, as director of Lionheart Books and
Bender Richardson White, has edited and produced even more than this for
the international book market.

Credits
Editor: Philip de Ste. Croix
Designer: Stonecastle Graphics Ltd.
Color artwork: Rod Ferring © Colour Library Books Ltd.
Picture Editor: Miriam Sharland
Production: Ruth Arthur, Sally Connolly, Neil Randles, Andrew Whitelaw
Director of Production: Gerald Hughes
Typesetting: SX Composing Ltd.
Color separations: Scantrans PTE Ltd, Singapore
Printed and bound by New Interlitho SpA, Italy

The vivid coloration on the head
and body of the Puss moth
caterpillar is a defensive
adaptation to deter predators
from eating it.

CONTENTS

Understanding the living world

How does an adult salmon find its way thousands of miles across open sea to the very river in which it was born in order to mate and produce offspring? What prompts wildebeest (a type of large African antelope) to migrate in their thousands across the Serengeti Plain in Africa, often with great hardship and danger to themselves? Why should a flea need to jump distances 200 times its own body length? How do bees communicate with one another in their hives?

To most of us, these do indeed read like miracles of life because we cannot readily explain them. However, this book sets out to answer such questions and to describe why these feats and achievements are a normal part of the struggle for survival among living things. And as you find out more about the abilities and behavior of our fellow animals and about the lives of plants, you will also appreciate that such miracles are everyday events in the natural world.

Honey bees may not seem very 'tame,' but they produce lots of honey, and they are less fierce than wild bees! Knowledge of bee behavior has helped bee-keepers to breed less aggressive, easier-to-handle bees.

This flea, smaller than a rice grain, is at the moment of take-off. It leaps to escape danger, or to jump on to a host.

An age-old scene: piglets take milk from their mother in a farmyard sty. Pigs were first domesticated over 8,000 years ago.

The hunter-gatherer lifestyle of early humans has given way to scientific, mechanized farming, like these rice-harvesters in Richvale, California.

After they have eaten the grasses in an area, or the dry season begins, wildebeest set off on long-distance treks to search for new pasture.

These piglets and their mother belong to the Tamworth breed. There are more than 300 breeds and varieties of pigs in the world.

Why should we study and try to understand the ways of living things? For our ancestors it was an essential part of their own struggle for survival. They lived by hunting wild animals and gathering wild plants. They had to learn where, when, and how to capture fish, shellfish, birds, and mammals, and to collect grain, berries, nuts, and fruits. An understanding of seasonal changes, migrations, defenses, camouflage, and mating behavior of animals was needed in order to survive.

As populations increased in size and more and more food was required, so agriculture developed. To domesticate animals and cultivate plants required an even greater knowledge of the ways of nature. Our ancestors had to learn which animals they could tame, how to bring them up and breed them, and how to care for them when they became ill. Plant seeds had to be harvested, sown, and nursed into growth.

The science of animal behavior

Today, biologists study animal behavior in the hope that it may tell us something about our own behavior and may help us to manage, conserve, and protect all living things. Throughout this book we shall compare and contrast the ways of life of other animals with our own. We shall also highlight the manner in which we have adopted some of the 'miracles of life,' such as the navigational skills of homing pigeons and the camouflage and mimicry of insects.

The *science* of animal behavior dates from the middle of the nineteenth century when the work of naturalists Charles Darwin and Alfred Wallace revolutionized biology. In 1859 Darwin wrote *On the Origin of Species by Means of Natural Selection and the Preservation of Favoured Races in the Struggle for Life.* This book changed ideas about evolution and prompted other naturalists to examine the ways in which animals interact with one another, with plants, and with the environment. Wallace developed ideas about evolution similar to those of Darwin, but also studied the distribution of wildlife. He attempted to explain how different creatures are adapted to different surroundings and why each part of the world has a unique mix of species.

Charles Darwin (1809-1882), here surrounded by pictures of birds and flowers similar to those that set him thinking about the process of evolution.

Alfred Wallace (1823-1913) collected animals and plants in South America and Southeast Asia, and sent specimens to European museums for examination and study.

Unlike anatomy – the study of the structure of organisms – and, to some extent, physiology – their functioning – the science of animal behavior involves the observation of living creatures. An animal behaviorist studies what animals do and how they do it. Then he or she tries to explain why they do it. What advantage does it have for the survival of the species? Studying animals in the wild is difficult. Fish, birds, and mammals must be tracked over great distances. Nocturnal animals have to be studied in the dark. Animal sounds must be recorded. Creatures must be captured in order to measure and weigh them. So there is a limit to how much one can find out. Some miracles of life will probably remain a mystery for a long time yet.

Pigeons can fly back to their home loft with amazing accuracy. Their abilities have taught us much about animal navigation, and our own magnetic sense.

A radio beacon has been harmlessly fitted to this Gray seal. Its radio signals are tracked by scientists, who can follow the seal's dives for food and its movements through the ocean all year round.

The shadow on this leaf is not another leaf behind, but a Japanese leaf-insect – one of hundreds of examples of animal camouflage evolved by both predators and prey.

Darwin made dozens of notebooks about his world travels, and the creatures and plants he saw.

Animals as machines

At first, animal behaviorists regarded our fellow creatures as mere machines. They believed that everything an animal did was the result of automatic reactions. For example, touch a cat's ear and the ear twitches rapidly. Then the cat shakes its head and scratches its ear with its hind paw. Shine a torch in front of a cockroach, and the insect immediately turns away. These are called reflex actions. We, too, have such automatic responses. Go to strike someone on the nose and they instantly blink to protect their eyes. Reflex actions usually have a safety or defense function.

Earlier this century, Russian scientist Ivan Pavlov and several American scientists showed that these reactions can be modified. Animals have the ability to learn by experience and to change their behavior to suit changing circumstances. A rat in a maze with food at the center will learn to remember which paths it explored which led to nothing until eventually it goes straight for the reward. Animals can indeed reason and solve problems as we can, as some of the facts in this book will highlight.

Ivan Pavlov (1849-1936) showed how animals could adapt their built-in behavior and learn from experiences. He called them stimulus-response reactions.

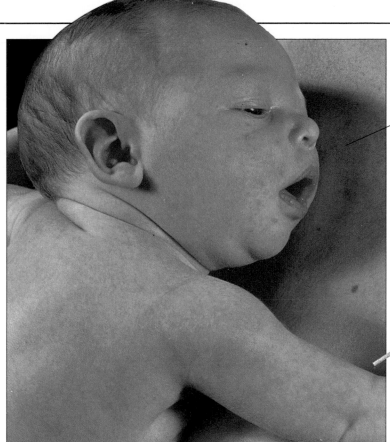

A newborn baby clings tightly to its mother. This behavior does not have to be learned. It is instinctive, or built in from birth. Gradually the baby learns to cling to people it knows, and to avoid strangers.

Swimming with a killer: the Killer whale, or Orca, is a deadly hunter. Yet in captivity, it can behave gently and learn many complicated tasks.

Are birds really 'bird-brained?' Recent tests show that they can learn to solve difficult puzzles requiring decision-making abilities, to get at the food inside.

In the rook's nest, the chicks automatically open their beaks wide, so that the parents will feed them. As they grow up, they no longer beg like this.

Animals also show instinctive behavior, which is activity inherited from their parents as special adaptations to their way of life. A young bird, on leaving the nest for the first time, will instinctively flap its wings and try to fly. A newborn baby, if touched on the cheek, will turn its head in search of its mother's nipple and milk to drink.

Throughout this book you will read about the special adaptations and behavior of animals and the characteristics of plants. In so doing, you should appreciate why it is so difficult, if not impossible, to create machines and devices that can perform as well as animals do. For instance, to create a computer that can play chess, do math, or address letters is one thing, but to build a computer that can learn by experience and make intelligent decisions is something else.

Plant power – making fuel for life

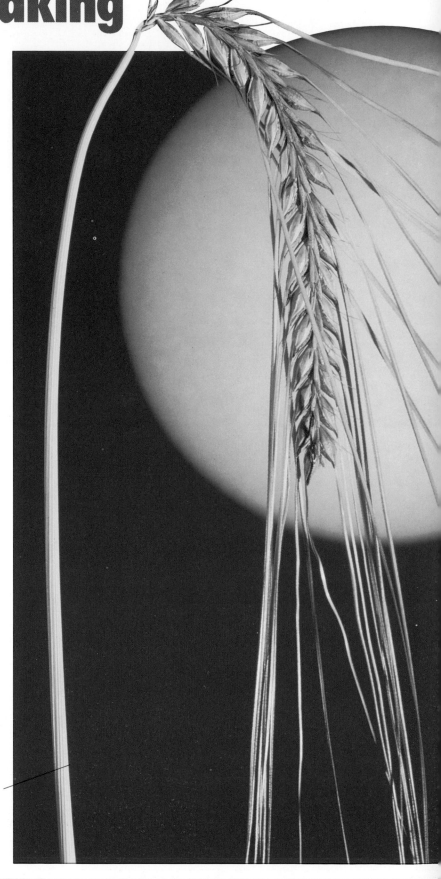

Almost all life on Earth depends on the Sun. Light energy from the Sun's rays is captured by plants, in a chemical process known as photosynthesis – the term is derived from the Greek words that mean literally 'building with light.' Only plants possess the green substance chlorophyll, which is at the heart of the complex chemical pathways of photosynthesis. Plants use the captured light energy to join together small, simple minerals and chemicals, absorbed from soil and air. These are assembled into much bigger molecules that make up living plant tissue. Some of these, like sugar in a flower's nectar, and starch in a rice grain, are themselves rich in energy. It is this energy that fuels the rest of life. One category of animals is the herbivores, which eat plants. They digest the plant tissues, employ the nutrients as building-blocks for growth and repair of their own bodies, and use the energy to power their own life processes. Another category is the carnivores, which eat other animals. As they digest their prey, they do broadly the same as herbivores – obtain body-building nutrients and energy. Decomposers such as fungi, certain microbes, worms, and mites get their nutrients and energy from the dying and dead bodies of animals and plants.

Honey bees feed on nectar and store any surplus as honey in the comb to feed the larvae.

A ripe ear of barley. The grains are rich in carbohydrates (sugars) and proteins. Cereal crops such as this provide food for herbivores.

The setting Sun, generating energy for use by plants to make their own food.

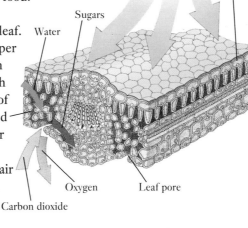

Section through a leaf. Chloroplasts in upper leaf cells contain chlorophyll which traps the energy of sunlight. It is used to combine water from roots and carbon dioxide in air to make sugars.

Upper leaf cells

Sugars

Water

Oxygen

Leaf pore

Carbon dioxide

Sheep are herbivores. They are efficient convertors of plant food into meat and milk which we may consume to provide fuel for our bodies.

Cotton fibers are long strands of cellulose, a carbohydrate made by plants. We cannot digest it, but the sheep have stomach bacteria that can.

FACT FILE

❏ Plants are not very energy-efficient in capturing light energy. Less than one per cent of the energy in sunlight ends up in the plant's tissues.

❏ Some plants have given up photosynthesis altogether. Greater broomrape is a pale yellow-red woodland plant that has no chlorophyll. It is a parasite, stealing nourishment from broom or gorse.

❏ Some life forms do not depend on the Sun. The sulfur gases that bubble out of deep-sea vents contain energy-rich chemicals. These fuel a strange community of bacteria, worms, crabs, and other deep-sea creatures, which live down there far from the Sun's light.

❏ Plant leaves absorb and use light mainly from each end of the light spectrum, the red and blue wavelengths. The green wavelengths of light in the middle of the spectrum are reflected from leaf surfaces rather than absorbed — which is why most leaves look green.

Finding food – from hunt to harvest

Animal life revolves around a few basic necessities. Finding food is the most necessary action of all. Any living thing is a potential meal for someone, and animals have evolved all manner of techniques for finding and consuming food. Hunters – from sharks to leopards – have good senses to help them locate their prey, speed to chase it, and large, sharp teeth to grasp and slice it. Since their fleshy meal is nutritious and easy to digest, they do not need to feed often. Many plant-eaters – from rabbits to deer – also have sharp senses and swift reactions. But these are mainly to escape predators, rather than find food of their own. Plant meals are relatively easy to obtain, but not so nutritious. Old leaves and tough grasses contain stringy, indigestible fibers. Even tender young leaves, shoots, and fruits must be well mashed to release their goodness (plant cells have thick cellulose walls that resist digestion). So a herbivore's teeth are flat-topped, while its head has strong jaw muscles for prolonged chewing. Hyenas, jackals, and others have a different lifestyle: they make a living by scavenging. They devour the old, sick, injured, or just plain dead. Their powerful teeth and jaws can shear gristle and crunch bone, processing parts of the carcass true predators cannot utilize.

One man and his tracker dog – a Pygmy from Zaire in Africa, who hunts small mammals, such as deer and rats, and gathers plants and fruits to eat.

A combine harvester collecting and separating the grains of barley – for people to eat – from the straw – which will be fed to farm animals.

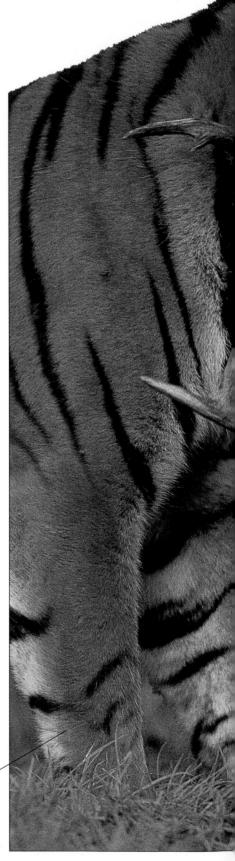

A tigress with her kill, a Hog deer. Only about 1 in 20 of a tiger's hunting attempts are successful. Large prey, like this, are choked to death with a bite to the throat.

An African wild dog on the prowl for an impala or gazelle on the Serengeti Plain, Tanzania. Wild dogs hunt in packs of up to twenty.

An African elephant uses the tip of its trunk to strip leaves and twigs from an overhanging tree.

❏ Animals that specialize in eating grasses and low-growing herbage, such as zebras and wildebeest, are called grazers. Those that pull leaves from bushes and trees are browsers – one of the best examples being the giraffe.

❏ Some large herbivores spend most of their lives eating and chewing. A horse grazes grass for up to 20 hours each day.

❏ A large snake such as a python uses up little energy, being a cold-blooded creature and asleep for much of the time. So a large meal like a goat lasts it for up to one month.

❏ Humans are omnivores – we eat most foods. With our plant-harvesting machines and farmed animals, we carry on the diet that our prehistoric hunter-gatherer ancestors obtained with their hands – picking berries and fruits, and using stone tools for catching prey.

❏ An elephant's diet of tough leaves and grasses contains so few nutrients, that, in order to sustain itself, it must eat 330lb (150kg) of food daily!

❏ Coal is 'food' for a blast furnace. Coal formed from plant matter that grew millions of years ago. As it is burnt, the chemical energy it contains – the result of photosynthesis – is released as heat.

Cannibalism – having a friend for dinner

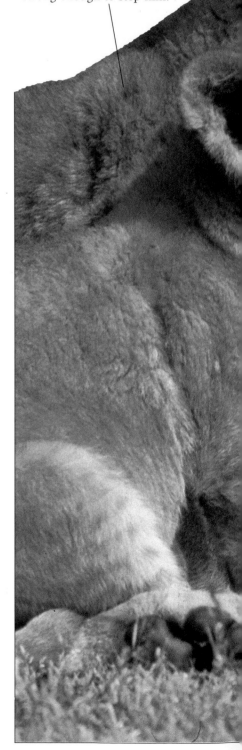

Young lions, or cubs, are dependent on their parents for food. But if a new male lion takes over control of a pride by defeating the old male, the newcomer may make a meal out of the cubs. The cubs' mother is not strong enough to stop him.

Most people prefer not to think about cannibalism, which means eating those of your own kind. But it has occurred in several human societies in the past, and it is surprisingly widespread in nature. In general, evolution has a problem with cannibalism. Imagine a group of animals that live and breed together, for their mutual benefit. Eating other members of the group means you are eating their genes – their hereditary material, which is passed from one generation to the next. The genes are the future of the group. By destroying them, you are helping to destroy the group's future, and so endangering your own existence! Yet killing and/or eating members of the same species has evolved in certain situations, usually for short-term advantage.

A backswimmer replenishes its air supply (a large air bubble) at the surface of a pond. When desperate for food, it will turn cannibal.

Sometimes food is so scarce that the need to survive outweighs the drawbacks of cannibalism. Little water bugs called pond backswimmers turn cannibal when this happens in a drying-up pond. Occasionally the need for a territory, which provides food or breeding space, is vital. Crows may eat eggs or chicks of other crows to drive away the parents and take the territory for themselves. Gulls also do this. It is a far cry from the vehicle wrecker's yard, where the mechanic 'cannibalizes' by taking the parts out of several broken old automobiles to make a whole, working one!

A Herring gull and a broken egg from a gannet's nest. Some pairs of gulls and gannets will eat the eggs of young of their own kind to take over the parents' breeding territories, in order to set up territories for themselves and their offspring.

By mating with the new male lion, the lioness helps him to pass on his own genetic material to the next generation of cubs.

House mice can produce five litters a year, each with up to seven young. When their population sizes become too big for the amount of food available, adult mice will kill some of their own young so that others may survive. This may happen every year.

Symbiosis – partners in life

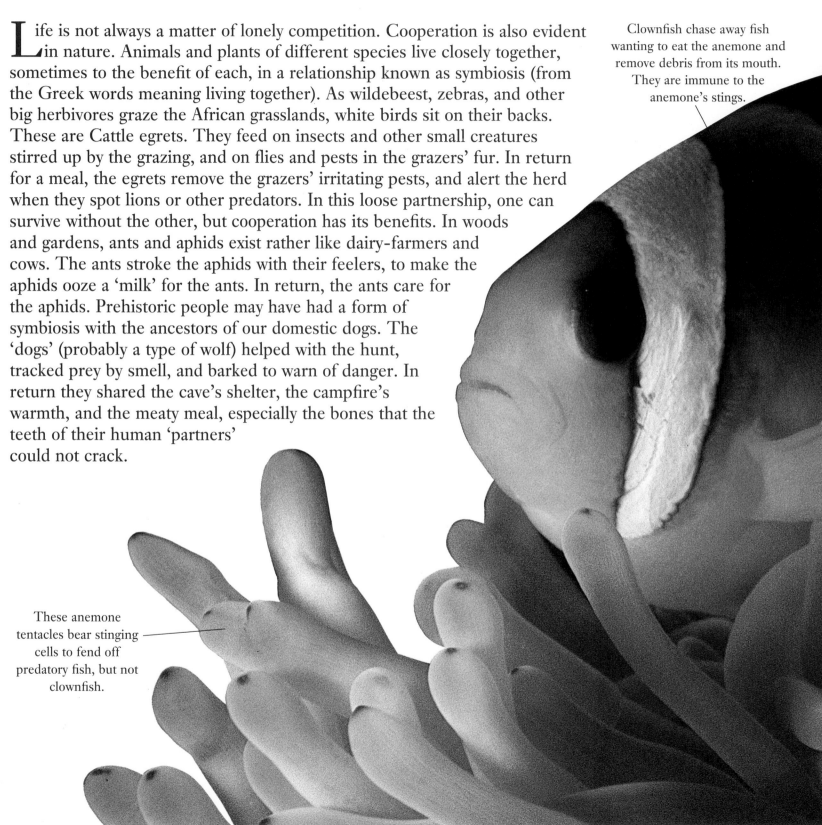

Life is not always a matter of lonely competition. Cooperation is also evident in nature. Animals and plants of different species live closely together, sometimes to the benefit of each, in a relationship known as symbiosis (from the Greek words meaning living together). As wildebeest, zebras, and other big herbivores graze the African grasslands, white birds sit on their backs. These are Cattle egrets. They feed on insects and other small creatures stirred up by the grazing, and on flies and pests in the grazers' fur. In return for a meal, the egrets remove the grazers' irritating pests, and alert the herd when they spot lions or other predators. In this loose partnership, one can survive without the other, but cooperation has its benefits. In woods and gardens, ants and aphids exist rather like dairy-farmers and cows. The ants stroke the aphids with their feelers, to make the aphids ooze a 'milk' for the ants. In return, the ants care for the aphids. Prehistoric people may have had a form of symbiosis with the ancestors of our domestic dogs. The 'dogs' (probably a type of wolf) helped with the hunt, tracked prey by smell, and barked to warn of danger. In return they shared the cave's shelter, the campfire's warmth, and the meaty meal, especially the bones that the teeth of their human 'partners' could not crack.

Clownfish chase away fish wanting to eat the anemone and remove debris from its mouth. They are immune to the anemone's stings.

These anemone tentacles bear stinging cells to fend off predatory fish, but not clownfish.

Stagshorn fern grows in the angle of tree branches, its roots gaining water and nutrients trapped in nooks and crannies in the bark.

A symbiotic association of an ant and a colony of aphids. The ant is stroking an aphid with one of its antennae, or feelers, to get it to release food.

Two Cattle egrets get their fill of insects from a wildebeest, one from its fur, the other from grass it has disturbed. Oxpecker birds do the same.

❏ In obligatory mutualism, both species have to be in partnership. One would find it difficult or impossible to live without the other. An example of obligatory mutualism is the yucca plant and Yucca moth from North America. The moth is virtually the only creature that can spread pollen from one yucca to another, so that their seeds can develop. The moth's caterpillars can only feed and develop in the ripening yucca flower. So moth and flower are unable to survive without each other. This partnership evolved over millions of years.

❏ In another type of cooperative relationship, commensalism, one partner gains from the arrangement while the other is not affected. The Remora or Shark-sucker fish hitches a ride from its host, and it may eat leftovers from the shark's meal. The shark is usually unaffected. Up to about eight such commensals will gather round a shark's mouth.

❏ Clownfish live in close harmony with anemones. The fish live among the stinging tentacles of the anemones, picking up and eating loose particles of food and receiving protection from larger predatory fish. They are immune to the anemone's stings. There is no indication that the anemones benefit from this intimate relationship and they can in fact live independently of clownfish.

Parasites – unthankful 'guests'

Have you ever been bitten by a flea, louse, or mosquito? These tiny blood-sucking insects are parasites – animals that feed or gain shelter from another kind of creature, known as the host. You are the mosquito's host! Parasites are usually much smaller than their hosts. They do not kill and consume them, as a predator eats its prey. Nevertheless, the host is harmed in some way by their presence. Unlike symbiosis, where both partners may benefit, parasitism is a one-way relationship. The parasite gains, but the host loses. The host's suffering can range from slight irritation to death. For example, the South American vampire bat (the parasite) slits a small cut in a cow's skin, and laps up a blood meal. The cow (host) is left with only a small wound. On the other hand, a heavy infestation of gut worms can kill the host animal. Plants can be parasites, too. Mistletoe sends 'roots' into its host tree to suck up the sap, depriving the host of valuable nutrients. Parasitism shows the delicate balance of the web of nature. If a parasite is too successful, its host gradually dies off, and so the parasite dies out too. If the parasite is not successful enough, its hosts manage to repel it, and it also dies out. It is a continual see-saw, which is very finely balanced. We often upset the balance by using medicines to kill parasites that are important to us.

A Herpes simplex virus (orange sphere) escapes from the nucleus of a host cell (green). All viruses are parasites. They grow only in living things.

A computer virus strikes, making text on a VDU screen go fuzzy. The virus is a packet of software that upsets the computer's operating system.

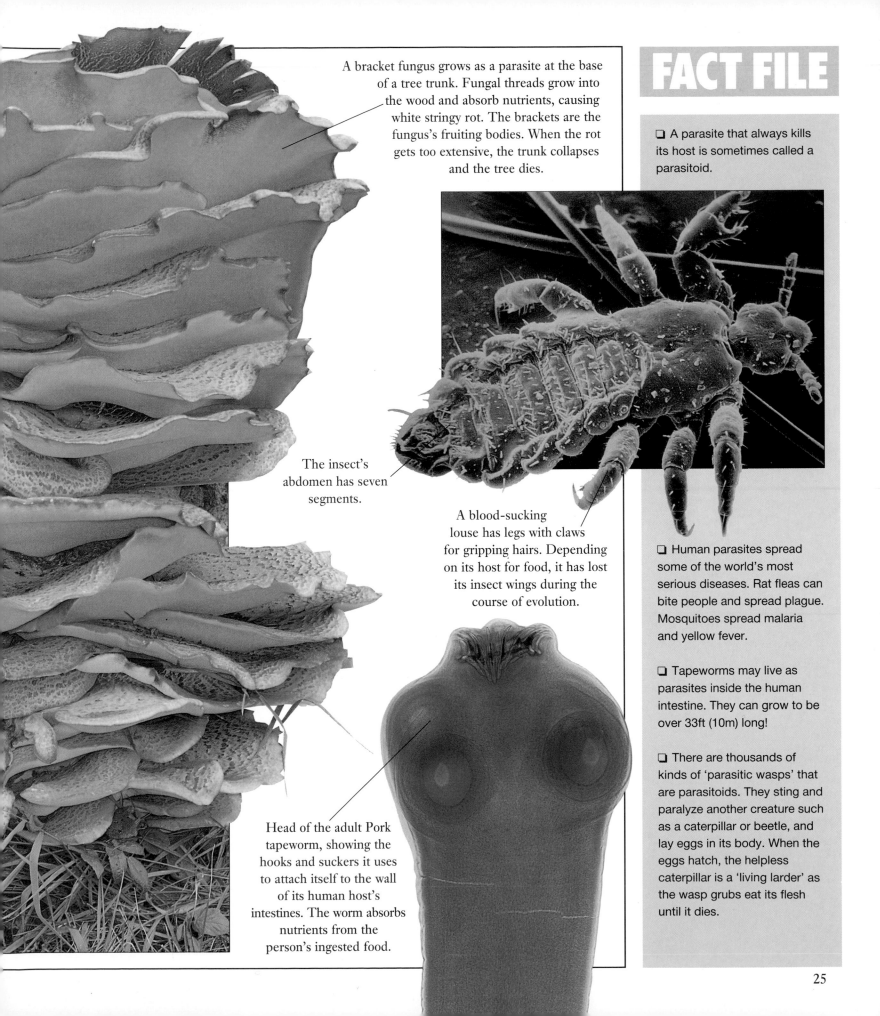

A bracket fungus grows as a parasite at the base of a tree trunk. Fungal threads grow into the wood and absorb nutrients, causing white stringy rot. The brackets are the fungus's fruiting bodies. When the rot gets too extensive, the trunk collapses and the tree dies.

❑ A parasite that always kills its host is sometimes called a parasitoid.

The insect's abdomen has seven segments.

A blood-sucking louse has legs with claws for gripping hairs. Depending on its host for food, it has lost its insect wings during the course of evolution.

❑ Human parasites spread some of the world's most serious diseases. Rat fleas can bite people and spread plague. Mosquitoes spread malaria and yellow fever.

❑ Tapeworms may live as parasites inside the human intestine. They can grow to be over 33ft (10m) long!

❑ There are thousands of kinds of 'parasitic wasps' that are parasitoids. They sting and paralyze another creature such as a caterpillar or beetle, and lay eggs in its body. When the eggs hatch, the helpless caterpillar is a 'living larder' as the wasp grubs eat its flesh until it dies.

Head of the adult Pork tapeworm, showing the hooks and suckers it uses to attach itself to the wall of its human host's intestines. The worm absorbs nutrients from the person's ingested food.

25

Animal architects – building for the future

Humans make all kinds of houses and living places. In traditional buildings we use the materials of the surrounding land. The Inuit people of the far north make igloos from ice blocks. People living near rivers and marshes construct wooden houses on stilts, thatched with reeds. Where there is plenty of clay, this is made into sunbaked housebricks. But we are only one of nature's architects. Insects, birds, and mammals are the main animal builders. They construct an incredible variety of structures, and they too use materials close at hand. Most animals make a nest or shelter to rest in, or in which to raise their family. The nest is often hidden somewhere, like the blackbird's cup-shape nest of twigs, grasses, and mosses hidden in thick vegetation. Other animals deliberately build in the open, such as the amazingly intricate flask-shaped nests of the weaverbirds. There are usually many nests crowded together, and the weaverbirds find safety in numbers with their continual noise and activity. Using building materials from nearby means the nest is automatically camouflaged, like the tennis-ball-sized nest of the Harvest mouse, woven from the stems among which it lives and feeds. Other nests are built to hibernate in. The dormouse collects dry leaves, grass, and moss to make a snug nest among tree roots. Here it sleeps the winter away.

Newly formed nest of a wasp, hanging from the underside of a roof tile. Several fertile females together make the nest then lay their little white eggs in the chambers. The wasps make the nest from dry wood, often from a fence post, which they chew to a pulp.

A male African weaverbird weaves its nest then uses it as a display area to attract a female. She will lay her eggs in the nest.

The male weaverbird first weaves a ring of grass fibers, knotting them securely to two supporting twigs.

A 10ft- (3m)-tall mound built by worker termites from soil particles cemented together with saliva and excrement. If termites were the same size as people their towers would be 5,000ft (1,500m) tall. The world's tallest skyscrapers are about 1,400ft (425m) high.

A Harvest mouse in its nest. The young mice are reared in the nest of grass fibers, which is attached to the stems of crop plants, providing a ready meal for the family.

Masai children and their dog stand outside their house, a hut made from branches, twigs, and mud baked hard by the Sun, nature's basic building materials.

❑ Our close animal relatives, the gorillas, make a nest platform of bent-over branches up in the trees, to sleep on at night. But the biggest male gorillas are too heavy and have to sleep on the ground.

❑ Termites are the greatest animal architects, for their size. These tiny insects construct huge hollow cooling towers more than 20ft (6m) high over their nests.

❑ A squirrel makes large rounded nests of twigs, called dreys, high in the branches. In spring it builds a nursery drey to rear its young. In autumn it makes a winter drey to keep out the cold weather.

❑ Male bowerbirds in Australia make bowers, structures of twigs and leaves shaped like mushrooms, conical tents, or fenced pathways, even decorated with colorful fruits and flower petals! The male dances and sings in his bower to attract a female. After mating, she builds the usual kind of bird's nest in which to rear her family.

❑ The male Mallee fowl of Australia digs a pit, fills it with leaf litter, then covers the lot with sand in preparation for the female to lay her eggs inside the 'compost heap.' Heat from the decaying plant material incubates the eggs. The birds regulate the temperature of the mound by adding or removing sand from the top.

Burrows and dams – digging down and building up

Soil may not seem nutritious to us. But to an earthworm, it is a complete meal. Earthworms eat their way through the soil, digesting the particles of old leaves and other nutrients, and making tunnels as they go. They are one of the commonest burrowing animals, and their tiny tunnels let air and water into soil, to improve its richness. Many larger creatures also dig tunnels and burrows. Some live in them. The mole feeds on earthworms and other soil creatures, and rarely comes above ground. Other animals use their burrows for shelter, safety, and raising a family, but go outside to find food. This happens particularly in grasslands and deserts, where there are few trees to give shelter or nest sites. Gerbils, kangaroo rats, and other desert creatures hide from the heat of the Sun in their cool, moist burrows, and emerge at night to feed. At the opposite extreme is the beaver family. These animals deliberately build a dam of sticks, stones, and mud across a stream, to flood an area. In the lake they create, they build a strong home called a lodge from boughs and twigs. Beavers are good swimmers and they can easily reach the lodge entrance, which is underwater. But the water keeps away predators such as wolves and lynx.

Beavers often build their lodges or homes in the middle of a pond. First they construct a dam around the lodge to control the water level in the living chamber.

A pair of European badgers emerge from their underground home, a sett. Their tunnels may go 60ft (18m) deep and 20ft (6m) down into the hillside.

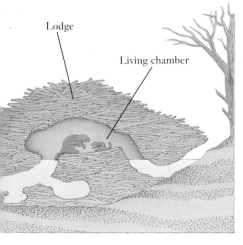

Lodge

Living chamber

Beavers make their dams from sticks collected from the riverbanks, piled up and often held together with mud.

Adult female beavers, like this one pulling along some construction material, are the most active lodge builders.

Shasta Dam, a hydroelectric power station in California. Water trapped behind the dam runs through pipes leading to turbines.

A mole emerges from its hole, showing its powerful, heavily clawed forelimbs used for digging its underground home.

❏ Some animals burrow extremely fast. The razorshell is a long, thin, two-shelled mollusk, shaped like an old-fashioned cut-throat razor. It burrows into the damp sand of a beach faster than you could dig it out!

❏ The Duck-billed platypus of Australia and the echidnas of Australia and New Guinea are the only kinds of egg-laying mammals (monotremes). The platypus lays its eggs in a riverbank burrow up to 50ft (15m) long, and the echidnas lay their eggs inside their ground burrows.

❏ Some animals dig their own burrows, others take over ready-made ones. Puffins usually nest in cliff-top burrows dug by rabbits.

❏ The longest man-made tunnel of any kind supplies water to New York City, U.S.A., from West Delaware. It is 105 miles (169km) long and just over 13ft (4m) wide.

❏ In parts of Borneo and Sarawak people still live in dwellings built inside the entrances to caves. The caves provide protection, and also house millions of bats that form part of the peoples' diet. In Roman times, poor people often lived in catacombs, the underground burial tunnels and chambers constructed beneath religious buildings.

Traps and lures – come into my parlor!

The leaf of a Venus fly-trap, a carnivorous plant. As a fly lands on the leaf and brushes against sensitive hairs inside it, the two halves of the leaf snap shut. The inner surface of the leaf secretes digestive enzymes.

Some predatory animals use speed and strength to catch their prey. Others set traps and hide in wait, tricking the prey and luring it to its doom. Almost every kind of trap invented by humans – whether to catch animals for us to eat, or study, or to destroy pests – has already evolved in nature. There are pits and trapdoors, nets and snares, and even glowing light-lures. Spiders are well-known trap-makers. Their intricate silken webs form a variety of beautiful patterns, from the spiraling orb web, to the sheet-type hammock web of the common house spider, to the cone shape of the deadly funnelweb. The larva of the ant-lion (a type of insect) is a pit-maker. It digs a circular pit in soft sand and waits, buried just under the surface at the bottom. It seizes ants and other creatures that tumble in and cannot climb out on the loose grains. Light is an effective lure, especially in the dark ocean depths, since some fishes recognize mates by the pattern of glowing lights. However, sometimes the light is not that of a friendly mate, but the lure of a deep-sea anglerfish whose huge mouth opens to suck in the victim. Plants, too, lure animals to their death by scents, or by the promise of a sweet meal of nectar. This is especially true of plants that live on poor soil, like sundews, since the digested prey provides valuable nutrients lacking in the ground. These are mostly minerals that are essential for metabolism.

A fly, attracted by glistening droplets on the tentacles of this Sundew leaf, becomes trapped – the droplets are sticky. The tentacles also secrete digestive enzymes.

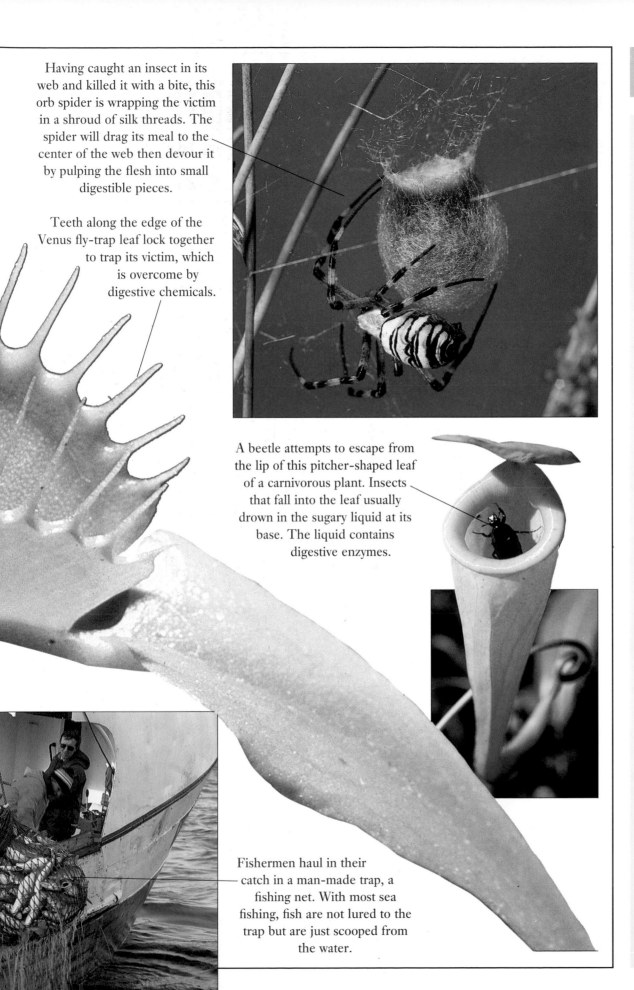

Having caught an insect in its web and killed it with a bite, this orb spider is wrapping the victim in a shroud of silk threads. The spider will drag its meal to the center of the web then devour it by pulping the flesh into small digestible pieces.

Teeth along the edge of the Venus fly-trap leaf lock together to trap its victim, which is overcome by digestive chemicals.

A beetle attempts to escape from the lip of this pitcher-shaped leaf of a carnivorous plant. Insects that fall into the leaf usually drown in the sugary liquid at its base. The liquid contains digestive enzymes.

Fishermen haul in their catch in a man-made trap, a fishing net. With most sea fishing, fish are not lured to the trap but are just scooped from the water.

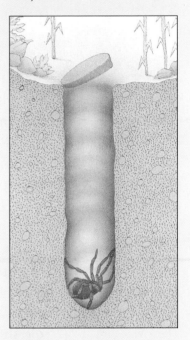

On the move – feet and legs, from sliders to leapers

A manned research submersible moves up and down through water by altering its buoyancy.

Evolution has fitted each animal to its surroundings and lifestyle – and the way it moves about is no exception to this rule. The need to escape from predators and to find food means that only a few animals, such as barnacles, are firmly fixed to one spot. From the crawling slug to the racing horse, animals use an amazing variety of movement methods. (Strangely, there are hardly any examples in nature of our most useful device to facilitate movement, the wheel.) The millions of species of arthropods ('joint-legged' animals), the biggest animal group of all, have legs for walking and running. These include the six-legged insects, eight-legged spiders and scorpions, and ten-legged crustaceans such as prawns and crabs. But legs are not compulsory for speed and agility. Snakes are legless yet they can swim, climb, and slide along with great ease. They move by curling the body into S-shapes that pass from head to tail, thrusting the snake forward. Some worms use the same technique. Water creatures push the water backward, to push themselves forward. They may row with their oar-like fins or flippers or legs, such as seals, penguins, and water boatmen. Or they thrash their tails from side to side, like marlins and sharks, or up and down, as whales.

A spider monkey hangs from a branch and supports itself using its prehensile tail.

Spider monkeys live in South America, the home of all primates with a tail that is capable of grasping (prehensile).

A gecko clings to a branch. Some geckos have special toe pads that allow them to cling to smooth surfaces.

A coconut palm germinates on a beach in Trinidad. The nut is the palm's means of spreading its offspring around the world; the nut is adapted to float on, and not absorb, water.

An adult eel slithers over the ground by wriggling its body like a snake. It breathes in air from water that it carries in its gills. It can stay alive out of the water for hours.

❑ The fastest animal on land over short distances is the cheetah, which has been timed at more than 60mph (nearly 100km/h). Over greater distances, the fastest land animal is the Pronghorn antelope, which can run for 1 mile (1.6km) at 42mph (67km/h).

❑ The fastest two-legged runner is the ostrich, which can race along at 40mph (64km/h). A world-class human sprinter, by comparison, runs at only 23mph (36km/h).

❑ Despite claims to insect speeds of more than 400mph (640km/h) for some dragonflies and bush flies, the fastest insect is probably the deerbotfly, which buzzes along at 35mph (56km/h).

❑ It takes a snail just over 2 hours to crawl a distance of 100yd (91m). A tortoise can cover the distance in just 22 minutes, and a hare in less than 6 seconds, which is faster than any person can achieve.

❑ The slow loris is so called as it slinks about in trees ever so slowly. This makes it difficult to see and therefore gives it protection from predators such as civets that live in the same forests.

33

Powered flight – true conquest of the air

Only four groups of animals have truly conquered the air: insects, reptiles (in the shape of pterosaurs, flying reptiles contemporary with the dinosaurs), birds, and bats. Others can swoop and glide, as shown on the following pages, but they cannot stay in the air for long. In nature, true flight relies on the ability to flap wings. As the broad, flat surface of the wing pushes air downward, driven by powerful muscles, the resistance of the air pushes the wing (and the animal attached to it) upward. This downstroke is the 'power' stroke. During the upstroke or 'recovery,' the wing is twisted or folded to make its surface smaller, so that the air puts up less resistance as the wing moves through it. The wings of insects are made of thin membrane, stiffened with hardened tubes called veins. Flies have two wings; many other insects, like dragonflies and butterflies, have four. Birds and bats have two wings. The bird's wing surface is formed by feathers, which are stiff and exceptionally light, and overlap to form an airtight surface. The bat's wing is supported by four very thin fingers, and the wing surface is a sandwich of skin and muscle and elastic fibers.

A Ruby-throated hummingbird hovers in front of a flower, feeding on nectar which it sucks up with its bill.

Hummingbirds can beat their wings up to 75 times a second.

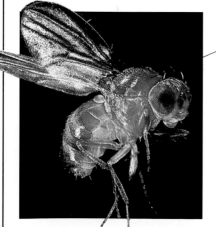

A fruit fly with its wings outstretched. Insects' wing muscles can contract much more rapidly than our own.

Primary feathers

Ribcage and breastbone

'Arm' bones

Wishbone

Secondary feathers

A bird's skeleton is similar to that of land vertebrates but the bones are honeycombed for lightness.

A brown bat in flight. A bat's wings act as an engine to propel the animal forward, as aerofoils to support it in the air, and, by altering their angle, as brakes to slow down flight and to help landing. Some bats use their wings to help catch airborne insects.

A Lockheed SR-71 'Blackbird' in flight. This craft holds the official world air speed record at 2,193mph (3,529km/h).

A longhorn beetle about to take off from a leaf. The forewings of beetles are hardened to form protective wing-cases for the delicate hindwings.

❑ The fastest movement in the natural world is that of a bird of prey, such as a Peregrine falcon, in a 'stoop,' diving on its prey. It can reach speeds of over 200mph (320km/h) in such a dive.

❑ In level flight, the Spine-tailed swift is one of nature's fastest fliers, with a speed of 106mph (170km/h).

❑ The fast-flapping wings of small fliers make a musical note, depending on the speed of their wingbeats. The high-pitched hum of a mosquito is the result of its wings beating at about 500 beats each second. The buzz of a bee is nearer 200 beats every second, while the hum of a hummingbird is about 80 beats every second.

❑ The heaviest flying bird is the Kori bustard, with a body weight of 40lb (18kg). The tiniest bird is the Bee hummingbird, which is about the size of a bee and weighs less than ⅛th ounce (1.6g). The largest bats are the flying foxes, with a wingspan of more than 30in (75cm) and weighing more than 3½lb (1.6kg). The smallest bat is Kitti's hog-nosed bat, with a wingspan of less than 6in (15cm) and a weight of under one-tenth of an ounce (2g).

❑ Butterflies are the most colorful fliers of the insect world. The largest of them, Queen Alexandra's birdwing, has a wingspan of 12in (30cm).

Gliding and soaring – riding breezes and thermals

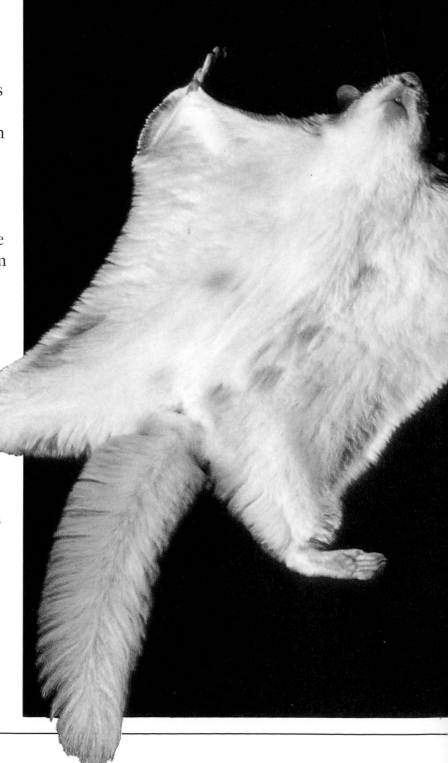

Although insects, birds, and bats are the only true fliers, the animal kingdom has many surprising gliders, swoopers, and soarers. Did you know that a snake from Southeast Asia can slither up a tree, and launch itself from the top branch into mid air? As it falls, it spreads it dozens of pairs of ribs sideways, so giving its body a flattened, ribbon shape. Then it swoops swiftly down through the air, curving into S-shapes as though it was on the ground to make its glide more effective. The 'flying' snake uses its ability to escape from predators or move swiftly after prey. Many other kinds of animals 'fly' – which is really gliding – in the same way, for the same reasons. Flying fish leap from the water and skim over the surface to avoid predatory fish. Certain kinds of frogs, lizards, squirrels, and possums also glide. Real fliers like birds and insects sometimes glide and soar without flapping their wings, in order to conserve energy. They use the wind blowing upward over cliffs and mountains, or the sea breezes rising over the coastline. In hot places like deserts, they spiral upward in funnels of warm air rising from the ground, which are known as thermals. Some seabirds, condors, vultures, and buzzards can remain aloft for hours, with just the occasional flap of their wings required to keep them on the move.

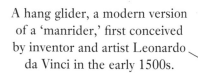

A hang glider, a modern version of a 'manrider,' first conceived by inventor and artist Leonardo da Vinci in the early 1500s.

With its limbs outstretched, a flying squirrel can glide between trees for up to 650ft (200m). The gliding surfaces are skin stretched between the tail base and hindlegs and from hindlegs to forelegs.

A radio-controlled model of a *Pteranodon*, a prehistoric flying reptile, in gliding pose. The model has a 15½-ft (4.6-m) wingspan, about half lifesize.

An Indian flying fox glides overhead. Despite its name, it is a bat. It has a wingspan of up to 80in (200cm), and glides through its forest home.

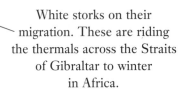

White storks on their migration. These are riding the thermals across the Straits of Gibraltar to winter in Africa.

❏ Flying frogs cannot in reality even glide properly. Their downward journey is more of a 'controlled fall.' In this respect, they resemble the Space Shuttle orbiter, which is designed to glide back to Earth to land. Its descent to the landing strip has been rather unkindly compared to that of a falling stone!

❏ Birds which are expert soarers and gliders have very long, narrow wings, like a sailplane. The albatross is the biggest example, with a wingspan of more than 10ft (3m). Albatrosses and swifts can stay aloft for many months without having to land, feeding and sleeping on the wing, and landing only to mate, lay eggs, and rear their young.

❏ There are three main kinds of gliding mammals. They are the flying squirrels (which are true squirrels), flying lemurs, and flying phalangers. The flying squirrel has two loose flaps of skin down each side of the body, called the patagium. When it leaps into the air, these flaps balloon out like the wings of a hang-glider. A large flying squirrel can glide over 300ft (almost 100m).

❏ Flying lemurs, or colugos, can glide even further. One swooped along for 450ft (136m) yet lost only 40ft (12m) in height in the course of this flight.

Exploration – finding out about the world

An artist's impression of the Voyager 1 spacecraft leaving Saturn after its encounter with the planet in November 1980.

Nearly all animals move about and explore their surroundings. It is part of the essential processes of finding food and shelter, avoiding overcrowding and danger, and locating a mate. Even creatures that seem fixed in one place in fact explore a little way. For instance, sea anemones shuffle about on their 'stalks' to find the best positions for catching small fish and other prey. All these animals use their senses to detect the world around them. Like us, some rely on sight and hearing, smell and taste. Birds explore mainly by sight, while bats 'hear' their way in the dark using their high-pitched squeaks and clicks as a form of radar to locate and avoid obstacles. Dogs build up a 'smell picture' of the places they visit. They know if they return to a place by remembering its smells, even if they cannot see or hear. Under the ground, moles sniff their way as they dig new tunnels and feel for prey with their delicate noses and whiskers. In water, smell and taste merge into one. Salmon can pick up the 'chemical fingerprint' of their home stream from many miles out to sea, as they head back upriver to spawn. Also in the ocean, whales may explore by an inbuilt magnetic sense that detects slight variations in the Earth's magnetic field, like a super-sensitive compass.

A female sand wasp drags a caterpillar she has killed back to her nest in which she has laid her eggs. She returns to the nest site by memorizing visual clues and landmarks around it. The caterpillar is food for her young.

Space exploration has involved unmanned craft landing on the Moon and on planets such as Mars and Venus, and transmitting pictures back to Earth. Manned craft have landed only on the Moon.

Voyager 1 was accelerated away from Saturn by the planet's gravitational force, taking it toward Uranus.

Captain James Cook (1728-79), the English explorer who was the first European to sail round the islands of New Zealand and land in Australia.

A Lesser black-backed gull. Many seabirds return to the same breeding site unfailingly each year. They find their way back mainly by sight.

❑ Some newly-hatched birds, like baby ostriches, can move and run almost as soon as they are born. They have the urge to explore their surroundings and they are called nidifugous, from the Latin words for 'fleeing the nest.' Nidicolous chicks, on the other hand, stay in the nest until they are full grown.

❑ Some of the most inquisitive and exploratory birds are seagulls, like Herring and Black-backed gulls. Their wanderings and curiosity have helped them to spread to new areas, like inland lakes and trash tips, where they can find food to sustain them.

❑ Some of the greatest oceanic explorers are the huge sea turtles. Individuals have been tagged and their travels monitored. They can swim at 18mph (29km/h), and they wander for thousands of miles between breeding seasons.

❑ Each fall, off the coast of Florida, thousands of spiny lobsters leave their holes in reefs and line up, one behind the other in columns of up to 50 individuals, and set off at great speed across the seabed toward deep water. There they spend the winter, safe from the pounding waves of winter storms and from predators. But in the cold waters food is scarce so, having used up their food reserves, they return to the reef the next spring to fatten up.

Homing instincts – the need to get back to base

Some animals put a lot of time and energy into setting up a home base – be it a nest, burrow, or shelter of some kind. Here the creature can rest, or feed, or rear young, relatively safe from danger. So when an animal is in peril, or tired, or wounded, its instincts (its natural, built-in behavior) urge it to head for home. A beaver threatened by a wolf quickly waddles and swims back to its lodge, finding its way by the sights, smells, and tastes of the landscape. A gerbil pursued by a desert fox remembers that it has dug several 'bolt-holes' where it can hide, and it dashes to the nearest of these. Once the immediate danger is over, the gerbil makes its way back to the main burrow and its nest. Even if an animal does not make a shelter or home, it is still an advantage to return to the place where it was reared. The very fact that the animal has reached adulthood means that its home area enjoyed conditions that were suited to its survival. This is why the instincts of salmon draw them back to their home streams, and why turtles visit the same beach to lay their eggs. If you were in trouble or felt threatened, where would you rather be – on a strange street, or back at home?

African wild dogs hunt, rest, travel, and breed in packs of between 2 and 20 individuals. When young are around, the pack stays in a home area.

Homing pigeons being released. The birds find their way back home over hundreds of miles using the Sun, Moon, and Earth's magnetic field as guides.

A fighter plane launches a guided missile that can home in on the heat from another plane's jet engines.

Adult salmon leap up rapids as they migrate upriver to the same spawning grounds in which their parents mated. To salmon, the waters of each spawning ground have a unique smell.

❏ One of the most powerful homing instincts is experienced by parents with young. If a mother mouse hears the squeaks of her wandering babies, at once she races after them, picks them up, and carries them back to the nest.

❏ Bees have a very strong instinct to return to the hive. Even if taken several miles away, they are usually able to find their way by using the Sun and other natural aids to navigation, back to their hive.

❏ Even the humble seashore limpet has a 'home.' This is a shallow hole it has scraped in the rock. Its shell fits snugly into the hole, so it has less chance of drying out in the sun or being dislodged by a wave.

❏ In one salmon hatchery, a freak flood washed the young fish out of their nursery pond, along an overflow ditch and into a nearby river. A few years later, during a dry spell, the grown-up salmon returned. They tried to swim up the now-dry ditch back to their pond!

❏ For more than 2,000 years, people have used rock doves to carry messages and to race for sport over distances of hundreds of miles. These 'homing pigeons' have an amazing ability to find their way back home. It appears they both navigate by the Sun and recognize landmarks remembered from their outward journeys.

Residents and migrants – home from home

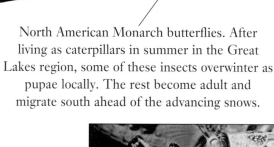

As fall approaches in North America, Europe, and other temperate lands, some animals prepare for the winter ahead. The residents (those who stay) may hibernate to avoid the cold, or simply scratch a living in the snow until spring. But other animals are preparing to travel. Birds gather in twittering groups on wires, tree branches, and building ledges, ready to fly south to warmer lands. Mountain sheep and deer move from above the treeline, down to the valleys of the lowlands. In the far north, caribou and other creatures which spend summer out on the tundra, are making for the shelter of the northern conifer forests. And in Africa, huge herds of wildebeest and zebra commence their trek to fresh grasslands, following the rainy season. These regular journeys – north/south, up/down, or following the rains and seasons – are called migrations. The migrants travel to avoid harsh conditions such as cold, drought, or intense heat, or to find plentiful food for raising young. In the spring, many birds such as geese and ducks, along with seals and whales in the sea, move from temperate lands to the far north, to take advantage of the rich but brief food supplies of the short northern summer. Some migrations are much shorter. Frogs and toads may travel only a mile or two in the spring, to their local breeding pond.

North American Monarch butterflies. After living as caterpillars in summer in the Great Lakes region, some of these insects overwinter as pupae locally. The rest become adult and migrate south ahead of the advancing snows.

A herd of wildebeest migrate across a river in the Serengeti in search of new grazing land. Many will die on the way through lack of food, drowning, or falling victim to predators.

Desert locust nymphs or young. Following conditions of overcrowding, these changed from living alone to gathering in huge swarms. On becoming adults, they will fly together and devour all plant-life as they find it.

Monarchs migrating south overwinter as adults in their millions in Florida and Mexico. Next spring, they return northward to mate.

❏ The champion migrators are Arctic terns. Some fly from their summer breeding grounds in the Arctic Circle, right around the world, to spend another summer in the Antarctic! The round trip is more than 22,000 miles (36,000km) each year.

❏ Adult eels migrate from the rivers of Europe, across the Atlantic Ocean to the Sargasso Sea, east of the Caribbean. There they breed. The young hatch and take three years to make the return trip.

❏ The largest numbers of migrators are in the swarms of desert locusts, which move across Africa and the Middle East. The biggest swarms contain 40 billion locusts. They land in an area, eat every scrap of vegetation, then fly on.

❏ In eastern North America, Blackpoll warblers leave Cape Cod in the fall. They arrive on the coast of northern South America, more than 2,500 miles (4,000km) away, after only four days! This non-stop migration over the sea is helped by strong following winds. They are flying at an average speed of about 26mph (42km/h).

❏ Commuting to work, going to school, or on vacation are all forms of human migration. Some are daily journeys, others weekly, or annual.

On reaching their breeding pond, these Common frogs have mated and produced masses of spawn – fertilized eggs in a protective jelly-like mass.

The 20,000-mile (32,000-km)-long migration of the Short-tailed shearwater. It leaves its breeding grounds off Tasmania in spring and spends the next seven months feeding on fish that abound in places in the Pacific and at times that the bird follows.

Navigation and orientation – Sun and stars, magnets and maps

Every fall, small birds such as warblers and swallows migrate from Europe, to spend a warm season in Africa. Even chicks born that summer, traveling on their own, sometimes complete the journey successfully. How do they find their way? When people set out on a long journey they carry maps, a compass, perhaps a starchart. Many animals have similar devices for finding their way, built into their bodies. Much of their behavior is instinctive – it is present from birth, and does not have to be learned. On a small scale, a digger wasp finds the way back to its nest burrow by sight. It recognizes features around the entrance, like pebbles and twigs. On a larger scale, the homing pigeon finds its way across hundreds of miles of unfamiliar countryside. Many experiments have been carried out to study animal navigation. For example, strapping a small magnet to a bird sometimes disrupts its homing abilities. It seems that some animals use a combination of methods to find their way about: visual landmarks, the positions of the Moon and stars in the night sky, a built-in magnetic compass, a 'solar compass' linked to the Sun's movements, as well as smell and sound patterns. Yet the details of how animals navigate are still one of nature's great mysteries.

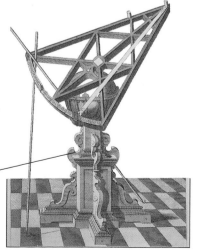

An astronomical sextant used by Tycho Brahe (1546-1601) to measure the positions of stars as seen from Earth. Brahe believed, incorrectly, that the Earth was the center of the Universe.

Mission Control at NASA's planetary exploration center in Pasadena, California. From here spacecraft are guided by radio signals to their onboard navigational equipment to Mars, Jupiter, Saturn, and beyond.

Swallows and martins on telephone wires. Like many migrant birds, these seem to have the ability to navigate by the Earth's magnetic field.

A Green turtle heads back to the sea. Turtles breed on land. On hatching, the young instinctively head straight for the sea.

❏ In one experiment, a small group of Leach's petrels (a type of seabird) were taken from their home on the coast of Maine, U.S.A., and flown by jetliner to England. Within two weeks of their release, they were back home, a journey of 3,000 miles (4,800 km)!

❏ Hawk Mountain, in the Appalachians of Pennsylvania, is named because of the many hawks that fly past each year, on migration. Each fall, up to 20,000 hawks and other birds of prey use the mountain as a landmark on their journeys south.

❏ The deepest sounds we can hear are about 20 Hertz (20 vibrations per second). Pigeons can hear sounds as low as 0.1 Hz (1 vibration every 10 seconds)! Such deep rumbles are made by waves crashing on shorelines and strong winds blowing over mountains. It is believed that pigeons are able to detect these sounds from many miles away and use them to navigate.

❏ Warblers and buntings, enclosed in planetaria with star patterns projected on to the ceiling, have shown an ability to recognize the changing position of certain stars in the night sky with the seasons. This may be one of the indicators the birds use to determine when to embark on their annual spring and fall migrations.

Rhythms of life – day in, day out, year after year

A graph showing how the depth of sleep waxes and wanes through the night. Dreams occur in between the high and low points.

Depth of sleep

Hours of sleep   1   2   3

What time is it? A watch or clock shows the exact time, but you probably have a general idea without looking at the clock – is it late morning, or past bedtime? A sense of time is vital in nature. Some flowers open their petals at the time when bees and other insects, which carry their pollen from one flower to another, are active. Otherwise the petals shut safely. Animals time their lives according to the main features of their surroundings. Like many mammals, we are used to the daily rhythm, being active during daylight and asleep in darkness. Most bats are night-active, because so is their main food – moths. To seashore crabs and snails, day and night are less important than the 12.5-hour cycle of the tides. They feed at high tide and hide at low tide. The 28-day lunar rhythm of the Moon is used by sea creatures such as palolo worms and Californian grunion fish, so that they all gather together at the same time and so improve their breeding chances. The yearly or annual rhythm is a major long-term cycle. In spring, warmer temperatures encourage plant growth, and this is the best time for animals to breed. Lengthening daylight brings many creatures into breeding condition. The daylight is received by the eyes, and in some animals by a special gland, the pineal, just in front of the brain. But the exact details of 'biological clocks,' like animal navigation, remain one of nature's mysteries.

This Evening primrose flower opens at about 6 p.m. and closes at sunrise.

Stonehenge, a prehistoric stone circle in England. We now believe the stones were set in this pattern to reveal movements of the Sun, Moon, and stars.

Electrodes attached to wires on this girl's head record the rhythms of electrical activity in the heart, brain, and facial muscles during sleep.

Young robins demand food from their mother. Like baby humans, the youngsters have a round-the-clock feed-sleep rhythm.

This tuatara lizard has a 'third eye' on top of its head linked to its pineal gland. It may regulate the reptile's internal clock.

❑ A 24-hour cycle, tied to patterns of daylight and darkness, is called the circadian rhythm. The term derives from the Latin words *circa* and *diem*, meaning about a day.

❑ Animals that are active by day and rest at night are called diurnal. Those that are active in darkness and rest by daylight are called nocturnal. Those that are mainly active at dawn and dusk are called crepuscular.

❑ In research, animals are kept in constant conditions, with no changes in light levels, temperatures, sound levels or other environmental 'cues.' The animals still keep their regular activity cycles, due to their internal biological clocks.

❑ Human volunteers living in constant conditions in a special laboratory tend to rest, sleep, and wake according to a daily rhythm. However many of them experience a slightly longer cycle, of about 25 hours. So, after three and a half weeks of the experiment, they have lost a whole day!

❑ In 1986, in the U.S.A, Robert MacDonald managed to go without sleep for nearly 19 days, the longest period on record. Most people sleep for between seven and nine hours each night. A new baby sleeps for 20 hours.

Dormancy and hibernation – sleeping through the bad times

Migration is one way for animals to avoid the harshness of winter, with its low temperatures and lack of food. But there are other strategies. Plants stop growing and become inactive, a state known as dormancy. A tree's buds stay closed, and flower seeds do not sprout, until the warmth of spring returns. Some insects become dormant in winter, often in a 'resting' stage of their life cycle, such as an egg or chrysalis (pupa). The body temperatures of 'cold-blooded' creatures such as lizards, frogs, fish, and insects are the same as the surroundings, so in cold weather they simply become too cold to move. Their body processes slow right down, a state known as torpor. This uses little energy, so they need no food to survive. Provided they do not freeze solid, they can usually survive the winter. Some warm-blooded animals like Gray squirrels, hamsters, and bears, hide in safe nests or dens and sleep for days at a time. They venture out only on milder days. Hibernation, as in marmots and dormice, is a specially deep winter sleep. The animal's body cools to temperatures as low as 35°F (2°C). Its heart beats slowly, and its breathing is shallow and irregular. It lives off stored body fat, until the warmth of spring breaks the hibernation.

New buds are vulnerable to late winter frosts. Fluffy fibers, as on the Pussy willow tree, help to protect the delicate buds.

The European brown bear dozes deeply in its den during severe winter cold. In milder periods it emerges to forage for food.

Many butterflies endure cold weather in the pupal stage. The caterpillar usually chooses a sheltered place to pupate.

Lithops plants are 'living stones' from desert regions. As gardeners know, these perennial succulents resist drought, but not frosts.

The insect food of many bats disappears in winter. So the bats hibernate in cool, moist places until spring, and a new supply of insects, returns.

A North American groundhog emerges cautiously from its burrow in late winter, after five months of hibernation. Unseasonally bright weather has roused it from its deep winter sleep. It is much less plump than it was in the fall, having used up much of its fat.

The wings and antennae of this Marsh fritillary butterfly are forming beneath the tough pupal skin.

Communication by sight – information from a distance

Our main sense, which tells us most about the world around us, is sight. Many other day-active animals also use their eyes a great deal. Vision is the sense that can help to attract a mate, signal to other members of the group, warn of possible danger, frighten away predators, or identify a potential meal – and all while these are some distance away. For example, the glittering metallic colors of the tropical Morpho butterfly can be seen by a potential mate from over half a mile (one kilometer) away. Birds such as peacocks and pheasants display their incredible plumage to the females during courtship. Group-living animals like horses and lions signal to one another by the position of their bodies, legs, tails, and ears. Birds feeding in a flock keep a lookout for the flash of colored feathers that means one of them has taken off, perhaps to avoid danger. At once, the whole flock whirrs away. In the same way, drivers on a freeway are alerted by colored signs warning of roadworks or an emergency ahead. Some creatures, especially caterpillars and butterflies, 'trick' their predators by flashing colorful circles when threatened. The spots look like the huge eyes of a hawk or cat, and the predator is so startled that it does not attack.

Red alert! Red spells danger for animals and humans alike. It is the color of spilled blood. The skull reinforces the message.

A *Dendrobates* arrow-poison frog from South America. The red skin warns other animals that the nerve poison it contains will paralyze them.

A peacock impresses a peahen with his amazing tail-fan display. The finer and healthier his plumage, the better mate he will make. Her chicks should inherit his strength and fitness, and so continue his line.

FACT FILE

❑ Visual communication is so important to humans, it is estimated that four-fifths of the information we take into our brains comes in through our eyes – as words, images, shapes, colors, and movements.

❑ A hungry chick in a nest gapes its mouth widely. When the parent sees the brightly-colored inside of the chick's mouth, it automatically pops food inside – even if the parent is itself almost starved.

❑ Some of the strongest poisons in the animal world are in the skins of arrow-poison frogs from Central and South America. The frogs' bright colors communicate this to a hungry bird, lizard, or snake!

The Peruvian *Pachylis* bug's astonishing colors mean: I taste horrible!

❑ Warning colors are well known to animals as well as humans. Among the most familiar are yellow or red stripes on a black background. These are shared by wasps and bees with their stings, caterpillars with horrible-tasting flesh, certain poisonous snakes, and symbols we use, like the one for radioactivity.

The European swallowtail has false 'eyes' and thin 'antennae' markings on its hind wings. A peck here from a bird is much less likely to injure the butterfly seriously.

Sound and smell – messages in screeches and stinks

Compared to sight, communicating by sound has several benefits. Messages can be sent through undergrowth or among the tree-tops, where the leaves would block a visual signal. This is why many kinds of monkeys chatter as they move and feed. They are keeping in touch with the members of their troop by sounds, so that it does not become too spread out. If a predator such as a snake appears, the lookout monkey screeches an alarm signal, and the troop scatters in all directions. The messages an animal sends by sounds can be quite complex, and they are usually meant for others of its own kind. For example, some monkeys have different alarm calls for predators on the ground, like prowling cats, or in the air, like circling hawks. If a monkey makes the first noise, the troop rushes to the treetops. If it makes the second, they hide in the lower branches. In contrast, smell messages are not as complicated as sights or sounds. But their advantage is that they remain active for hours or even days after the sender has gone. Cats, dogs, and other creatures leave smell marks around their home range. These territorial 'signposts' inform others that the area is occupied.

A male toad-treefrog calls in a gloomy Trinidad forest, at the start of the rainy season. When the female answers, the two get together to breed in a fresh pool.

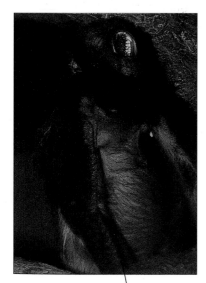

Red howler monkeys make some of the loudest sounds in the animal kingdom. Their dawn whoops tell other troops about their location in the forest.

The male Atlas moth's feathery antennae pick up the airborne scent sent out by its partner, which may be over a mile away. This scent is known as a pheromone.

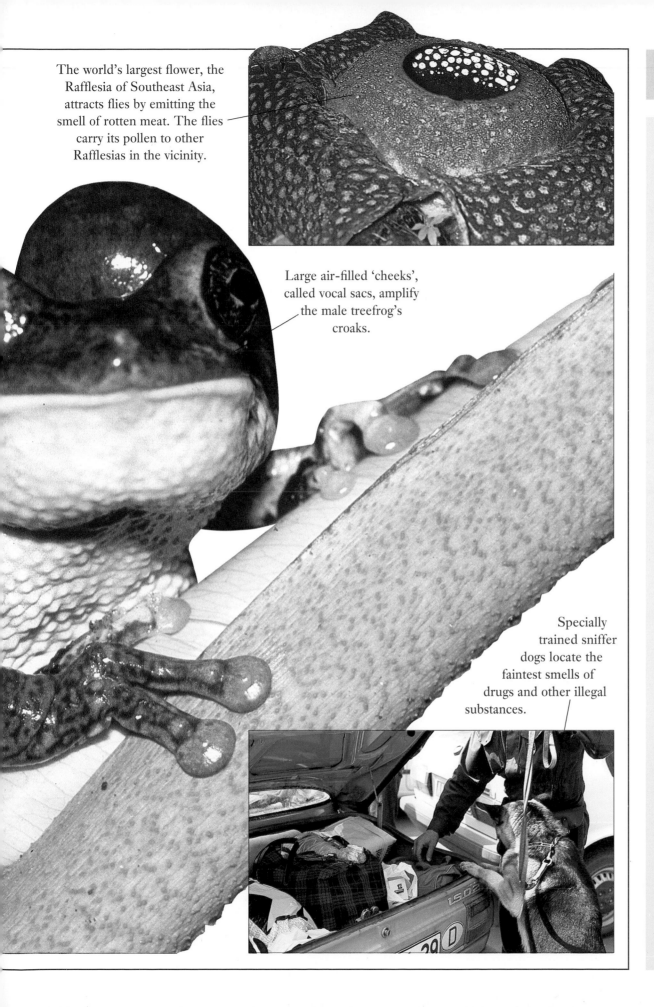

The world's largest flower, the Rafflesia of Southeast Asia, attracts flies by emitting the smell of rotten meat. The flies carry its pollen to other Rafflesias in the vicinity.

Large air-filled 'cheeks', called vocal sacs, amplify the male treefrog's croaks.

Specially trained sniffer dogs locate the faintest smells of drugs and other illegal substances.

❑ Humans do not rely much on smells as methods of signalling, compared to sights and sounds. So it is difficult for us to appreciate what some animals can smell. Dogs have a sense of smell 1,000 times more sensitive than our own.

❑ Certain male moths can detect the special mating scent of the female of their species from over 3 miles (5km) away.

❑ One of the loudest sounds made by any living thing is the deafening grunt of the Blue whale. It has been measured at over 150 decibels (units of loudness). By comparison, a jet engine rates at around 120-130 decibels.

❑ Cricket and grasshopper songs may sound much the same to us. Analyzed by computer, they are quite different – and the insects can tell between them. In fact, what was thought to be one species of grasshopper, from its appearance, turned out to be two species – each with a slightly different song.

❑ Some birds have 'dialects' or 'accents' in their song, like the accents of people from different areas. In a study in Wales, U.K. experts could identify which valley a chaffinch came from, by its song. In North America, the willow warbler, wood warbler, and chiffchaff look very similar, and are best distinguished by their calls.

Animal language – talking in sounds, postures, and gestures

Have you ever scolded a pet puppy for being naughty? It probably cowered, ears and tail down. The puppy was 'talking' to you – not in words, but by body language. The way it positioned its face, body, and limbs showed that it accepted you as the boss. You are the 'leader of the pack.' People use body language all the time, especially facial expressions. They smile, frown, shake their fists, or jump for joy. Animals also use body language, from gorillas and baboons to bees and spiders. A dog bares its teeth at a rival, a horse puts its ears back from fear, and a bull paws the ground with its hoof when angered. Wolf pack members communicate using at least 20 common postures and gestures, with different positions of the face, ears, back, legs, and tail. The most complicated language of all is our spoken language. We string together letters, words and other symbols in a special order each time, to make up long and complex messages. Creatures like whales and dolphins 'sing' strange songs of groans, wails, screams, grunts, and clicks, that sound like a language. But scientists have not been able to translate it or break the code to communicate with them.

Is this chimpanzee deep in thought? This is our human interpretation. Yet it may be resting, or – from its hunched posture – perhaps even feeling cold!

❑ The Humpback whale sings one of the most varied of whale songs. Sounds travel well in water, and its eerie wails can be heard more than 200 miles (320 km) away in the ocean.

❑ Chimpanzees and gorillas cannot talk like us because of their voice-box structure, but they can learn sign language. Some chimps know more than 200 signs, and join two or three signs together into a simple 'sentence.'

❑ No one knows when humans began to develop such a complicated spoken language. The hyoid (a bone from the voice-box area) has been found in a fossilized Neanderthal skeleton 60,000 years old. It suggests those people could speak, if their brains were intelligent enough.

❑ The male European marsh warbler can mimic the songs of more than 70 other birds, as well as making its own.

❑ We must be careful to understand the real message an animal sends with its body language, and not confuse it with our own meanings. A chimpanzee that looks to us as if it is 'smiling' is really exposing its teeth from fear. And when a male horse paws the ground, it is not counting, but either frustrated or ready to charge!

The African wild dog's snarl displays its ferocious set of teeth, as though saying: 'These will bite you, if you don't back off!' Its jaws can crush bones.

Bottlenosed dolphins produce a stream of squeaks, clicks, squeals, and other sounds as part of their means of communication.

In the Honey bee's dance, the number of body-waggles tells hive-mates the distance to nectar-laden flowers.

The Eastern meadowlark's long whistling notes, *tsee-you tsee-ear*, proclaim its territorial ownership.

Echolocation – seeing with sounds

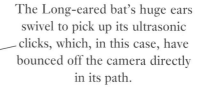

The Long-eared bat's huge ears swivel to pick up its ultrasonic clicks, which, in this case, have bounced off the camera directly in its path.

Have you ever heard the clicks and squeaks of a bat as it hunts flying insects at dusk? Many animals make sounds that are too high-pitched for most of us to hear. Children can sometimes detect them, since our ears are more sensitive to high-pitched sounds when we are young. Animals use these sounds, called ultrasound, to find their way about and locate food, even in complete darkness. The sounds spread out from the creature in a continuous stream, and they bounce off nearby objects, like the echoes you hear when you shout at a faraway cliff. The animal listens to the detailed echoes coming back, and detects how strong they are, and how long they have taken to return. From their pattern, it can work out the distance, direction, and size of objects around. This system of 'seeing' by sound is called echolocation. It was thought to be rare, but researchers are finding more and more animals that use it. Bats are among the experts, sending out dozens of ultrasound pulses every second as they zero in on a moth. Whales and dolphins use echolocation in the water – especially river dolphins that live in the muddy waters of the Amazon, Indus, Yangtze, and other great waterways.

The moth, detected by the bat's sonar, is now earmarked as a future meal. The strength of the returning echoes indicates the moth's size.

Radar systems use radio waves in the same way that bats use ultrasound. Each symbol and label on this display screen shows an airplane within about 60 miles (100km) of the radar tower.

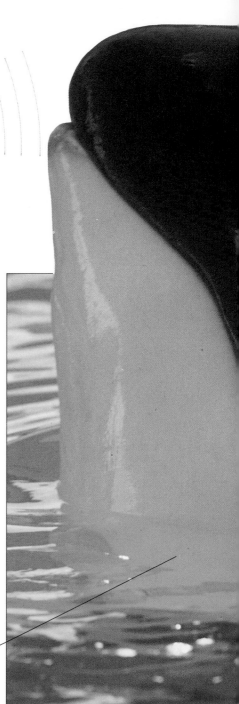

The Killer whale, or *Orcinus orca*, makes underwater squeals, honks, and gunshot-cracks as it communicates with its group members. These sounds help them to locate their prey.

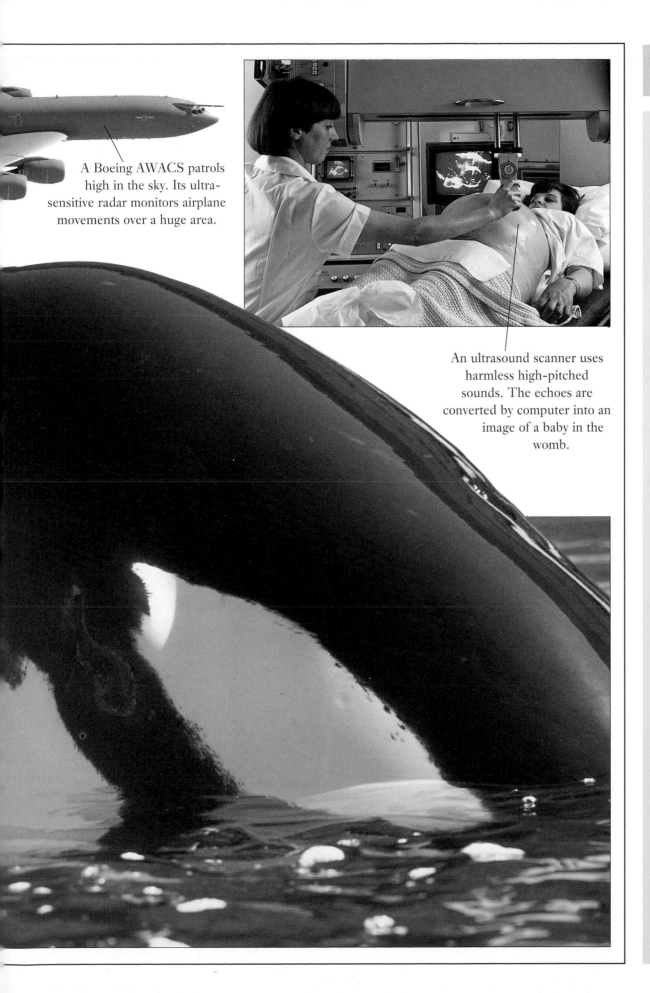

A Boeing AWACS patrols high in the sky. Its ultra-sensitive radar monitors airplane movements over a huge area.

An ultrasound scanner uses harmless high-pitched sounds. The echoes are converted by computer into an image of a baby in the womb.

Territorial marking – keep out of my patch!

At dawn and dusk, birds sing loudly from their regular perches and posts. They are telling other birds of their presence, and that their patch of land – their territory – is occupied. Rivals keep out! Numerous animals have territories, especially birds and mammals, and particularly during the breeding season. They defend the territory against others of their kind. The territory may be a small place to rear young, as with the nest sites of seabird colonies such as gulls. It may be a larger area that provides food for the family, as with many backyard and woodland birds, and lions and wolves. Sounds are one way of proclaiming territorial ownership, as in the birds' dawn chorus, and the howler monkeys of tropical America. Another method is to mark the territory's boundaries with smell messages, such as urine, droppings, or special fluids made in scent glands. The advantage of smell signs is that they remain for hours or days after the sender has gone. The tomcat who sprays his pungent-smelling urine at strategic places around his territory is a familiar example. Creatures such as lions patrol their boundaries and roar at neighbors. Real fights over territories, resulting in injury or death, are rare in nature. Usually rivals keep away, or merely threaten the owner with a visual display and frightening sounds.

This lioness keeps her claws sharp on a handy tree, indicating her presence near the border of her home range. The male lion does most of the pride's defense work.

In the breeding season, a robin may threaten and even peck any bird-like red object, believing it to be a rival robin-redbreast in its territory.

STRICTLY PRIVATE
Keep to footpath
unleashed dogs
will be shot.

Bright colors signal to rivals on the reef. This butterfly fish's body is, in effect, a stripy territorial flag.

The Mule deer has scent-making glands in the fur in front of its eyes, for smell-marking its home area. It rubs the scent on twigs and grasses.

Some humans are more territorial than their animal neighbors. In nature, the animals would shout or display first, and attack last!

Smelly urine and droppings produced by the lioness ward off adjacent lion groups.

❏ Many deer leave their droppings at special latrine sites, to mark their territory. At some long-used sites the droppings may make a pile more than 10ft (3m) high.

❏ One of the most valuable scents in the world is musk, which is an ingredient of many expensive perfumes. It is a jelly-like substance that comes from a gland in the rear belly of male Musk deer, which live in eastern Asia. The musk is dried to a powder. In some areas an ounce of musk is worth more than an ounce of gold!

❏ A special type of territory, called a lek, is a tiny area for which males compete by displaying their strength and stamina. The male possessing this type of territory, is most likely to mate with females. Sage grouse and African kob (a type of antelope) have breeding leks.

❏ Territory size varies, often depending on the richness of the food supply. Tiger territories vary from 8 square miles (20km^2) in Indian lowland jungle, where there are plenty of prey animals, to over 50 square miles (125 km^2) in the high hills.

❏ Some smells are made not to repel, but to attract. The male Emperor moth is supposed to be able to smell the mating scent of the female from over 3 miles (5km) away.

Threat and submission – hawks and doves

In the struggle for survival, each animal is trying not only to protect its own life but also to produce lots of offspring and thereby ensure that its genetic or hereditary material continues. Some do this by being aggressive, and others submissive. So within a population there are 'hawks' and 'doves.' When individuals confront one another, they adopt a characteristic display. Threat displays may be given to rivals in the group, as when male deer challenge each other for control of females, or baboons keep newcomers out of their group. The creature aims to look as large, strong, and fierce as possible, so that others back down before a real fight develops. So it stands impressively big and tall, and it may fluff out its feathers or fur to look even bigger. It makes frightening noises, such as growls or roars. And it shows off its main weapons – cats and dogs open the mouth to reveal fearsome teeth, horses kick out with their hooves, and deer and antelopes lower their heads to display their antlers and horns. Opposite to this is the submission or appeasement display, where the animal 'gives in.' It may cower or crouch down to look small, hide its teeth or claws or horns, make whimpering or whining noises, and look away, so as to be as unthreatening as possible.

On the steep, crowded rocks of a gannet nursery, a parent defends its chick by striking out at intruders who have mistakenly landed too close.

This Snow leopard threatens to attack. Its fearsome spear-like canine teeth are bared and ready, and its eyes half-closed for protection.

How did the Fire-bellied toad get its name? When at risk, it flips over and shows its red underside. A frightening sight – and a warning about its poisonous skin, too.

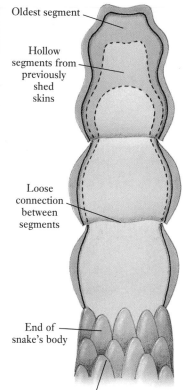

Oldest segment

Hollow segments from previously shed skins

Loose connection between segments

End of snake's body

The rattler's rattle consists of loosely linked old tail segments that stayed on when the snake shed its previous skins.

Worried by the photographer, this crab turns to face the threat, readies its pincers to inflict a bite, and rears up to look as intimidating as possible.

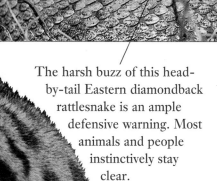

The harsh buzz of this head-by-tail Eastern diamondback rattlesnake is an ample defensive warning. Most animals and people instinctively stay clear.

Defensive reactions – from fighting back to playing dead

If a sleeping pet cat is suddenly disturbed, it leaps in the air, arches its back, makes its fur stand on end, shows its teeth, and hisses loudly. This is a defensive reaction. The cat tries to look as big and fearsome as possible, to frighten away any animal that may try to attack it. Some defensive reactions are similar to the threat displays described on the previous page. However the defense usually works not only against other members of the same species, but also against a wide variety of animal enemies. The cat's reaction is mainly visual, and visual signs are more likely to keep the opponent from coming too close. Other creatures use different defenses, especially when the enemy comes too near. Ants and beetles squirt or spray harmful chemicals that sting the enemy. The skunk is famous for its foul-smelling spray, and many other creatures, from caterpillars to birds, defend themselves with horrible smells. Well-armed creatures, from sowbugs to hedgehogs, armadillos, and pangolins, roll up into a ball that the enemy cannot open. One of the strangest defensive reactions is to 'play dead,' that is, to feign death by lying limply, without moving. Insects, birds, and mammals such as possums and sloths do this. The attacker usually wanders away!

Before actually squirting its horrible-smelling fluid, the Striped skunk raises its back legs and tail as a warning.

Get too close to an Australian frilled lizard and it rears up, spreads its frill wide to look much bigger, opens its mouth and hisses wildly, then races off on its rear legs!

The shieldbug's common name of 'stinkbug' comes from its habit of ejecting a fluid with an awful smell, when molested. These two are otherwise busy, mating.

With horny skin plates overlapping like roof shingles, the curled-up Indian pangolin presents a formidable defense to predators. This nocturnal mammal eats termites and ants. Millions of years ago, some dinosaurs had similar armor-plating.

FACT FILE

❏ The Giant petrel, a seabird, vomits up an awful-smelling oil and spits it at intruders. This is why old-time sailors called these birds 'stinkers.'

❏ The saying 'playing possum' comes from the oppossum's habit of lying still and limp when in danger, feigning death.

❏ The brittlestar, a type of starfish, is a champion at the defense called 'auto-amputation.' If a predator grabs one of its arms, special muscles in the arm contract to make it break off! A new arm soon grows. Crab legs and lizard tails can be shed and regrown in the same way.

❏ Plants have various defenses, such as spines and harmful chemicals. If you touch the tiny hairs on a stinging nettle, these break and release a stinging chemical. In nature, the stings put off plant-eaters such as cows, deer, and rabbits.

Weapons – armed to survive

Compared to other animals, humans do not have any impressive or dangerous weapons. We lack big fangs, pointed tusks, long horns, sharp claws, jabbing hooves, or a poisonous bite or sting. However, our intelligence has allowed us to develop tools as weapons. Some of the first tools were wooden and bone clubs, and sharp stone hand-axes and scrapers, for killing, skinning, and chopping up animal prey. Early kinds of humans such as *Homo erectus* used these more than one million years ago. They needed them, too – because most animals, when attacked, will fight back with whatever weapons they have. Our close relatives the apes and monkeys have long canine (eye) teeth and some possess sharp nails, for biting and scratching. Zebras and horses kick out at opponents or try to bite with their sharp incisor (front) teeth. In elephants, walruses, boars, peccaries, and some deer, like Chinese water deer, certain teeth grow long and stick outside the mouth. We call them tusks, and the animals jab and slash with them when threatened. Even the normally gentle giraffe can kick with its powerful legs, and swing its long neck and heavy head like a huge battering ram. These are all physical weapons. Some animals, plants, and fungi also have chemical weapons - stings and poisons. Less than one ounce (about 25 grams) of the 'flesh' of the deathcap, the most poisonous mushroom known, can kill a person.

Male Southern elephant seals fight to try and take charge of a stretch of beach, and the females on it. Unusually for animals, these fights may cause serious injury.

A Stag beetle's 'antlers' are outsized jaws. Males wrestle with them to win a female, but the jaw muscles are too weak to bite.

The main weapons of the innocent-looking comb jelly are whip-like sticky tentacles for catching prey as they swim innocently past.

A Yellow baboon threatens a troop rival to establish its status, baring its chief weapons – the dagger-like canine teeth.

A bull elephant seal can weigh over three tons, making it a truly heavyweight opponent that will fight fiercely.

❏ The longest elephant tusk ever found measured 11ft 5in (3.5m) along its curve. Elephant tusks are huge upper incisor teeth. Prehistoric mammoth tusks were even longer, more than 16ft (5m) in length.

❏ The longest horns are grown by the water buffalo of India. The biggest set was 13ft 11in (4.24m) measured around the curve and across the forehead, from tip to tip. Texan longhorn cattle have horns almost as big.

❏ One of the strangest tusked animals is the narwhal, which is a variety of toothed whale. Its spiral-patterned tusk is a greatly enlarged left tooth. Only males have the tusk, which can grow to 10ft (3m) in length.

❏ One of the few poisonous mammals is the platypus. The male has a poison claw, or 'spur,' on his ankle. Another is the shrew, which has poisonous saliva.

❏ A small octopus with a body the size of your fist, the harmless-looking Blue-ringed octopus of Southeast Asia and Australia, has one of the most powerful poisons in the animal world. One bite contains enough poison to kill seven people. The octopus tends to use this weapon only in self-defense.

Camouflage – fading into the background

Looking like a miniature dinosaur, the Three-horned chameleon from Africa changes color to match the background environment of the moment.

Out of the glare of direct sunlight, the stripes of this African zebra merge with the dappled shade cast by the thorny woodland edge. It needs to avoid being spotted by enemies.

Trickery and deceit is a vital part of life for many animals. They are camouflaged – colored and shaped and patterned to blend in with the background, so that it is difficult for enemies to detect them. Many butterflies rest among leaves with their wings folded to hide the bright patterns on the upper sides. The dull browns, greens, and grays of the lower surfaces merge in with the vegetation. Being camouflaged as something very common, like a green leaf, means that predators have less chance of finding you. Crickets, grasshoppers, bugs, beetles, treefrogs, and tree lizards are some of the animals that 'hide' in this way. Another method is to resemble something that is not nutritious. The eggs of the plover, a shore bird, look just like the pebbles among which they are laid, and the Dead-leaf cricket goes unnoticed among the brown leaves on the forest floor. People use camouflage, too. Warships are painted 'battleship gray' so as to be less obvious at sea. Soldiers wear mottled green and brown clothes in wooded countryside, sandy-colored khakis in the desert, and warm white suits in snow and ice.

The bush cricket's body is colored and shaped like one of the surrounding leaves, even down to the pattern of 'leaf-veins' along its side.

Ptarmigans are the only birds that molt their brownish feathers in the fall and grow white winter plumage, specifically for camouflage in the snow. This is a Rock ptarmigan.

Early spring leaves, just emerged from their buds, are often pale greeny-yellow and soft-looking. So are these Brimstones, one of the earliest of spring-flying butterflies.

FACT FILE

❏ The camouflage champion is the chameleon, a type of lizard. In seconds, it can change its skin color to match the surroundings, from almost black to nearly white, with all kinds and patterns of reds, blues, and greens in between.

❏ Another camouflage expert is the plaice, a flatfish. It can make its skin look yellow and sandy, or dark and blotchy, depending on the sea bed on which it rests.

❏ A fish that has been called 'the world's most poisonous animal' is camouflaged as a weedy lump of rock. This is the stonefish of Australia. The venom in the spines on its back can easily kill someone who accidentally treads on it in the shallows.

❏ One strange camouflaged creature is the Bird-dropping caterpillar, named because it resembles the droppings (feces) of a bird — something that most animals avoid!

❏ The way an animal moves adds to the camouflage effect. Some stick insects, twig-like caterpillars, and tree snakes sway in the breeze, to match the swaying leaves and branches around them.

❏ The Tawny frogmouth, an Australian bird, hunts insects at night. By day it sits still at an angle on a tree. Its mottled browny-grey feathers match the bark, and it looks just like the stump of a broken branch!

Mimicry – the harmless pretending to be harmful

If a small yellow-and-black striped insect flies near, people usually keep out of its way. But the insect may not be a wasp, with a painful sting. It could be a hoverfly, which has no sting. This is an example of mimicry, when a harmless animal is colored and patterned to resemble a harmful, distasteful, or unpalatable one. Other creatures learn to avoid the harmful animal, with its bright and obvious warning colors, and so they also avoid the mimic. Mimicry has evolved in many groups of animals, from flatworms and seaslugs to amphibians and birds. It is especially common in insects, spiders, fish, and reptiles. For example, a small fish, the Cleaner wrasse, swims around much larger fish and picks pests and parasites from their mouths and gills. A cleaner mimic, with the same coloration and the same 'swim-dance' as the cleaner, also swims up to bigger fish – but then takes a bite out of them! Mimicry works well provided there are not too many mimics and they do not become too common. If this happens, animals who attack them will find a tasty meal, and not horrid-tasting flesh or a venomous bite or sting. After a time, the protection given by the warning colors will no longer work.

Beetles lack stings. But this wasp-beetle gains protection by resembling a wasp. A bird scanning the buttercups for a tasty morsel is likely to avoid it.

The male Peruvian swallowtail is one of a group of very similar-looking mimic butterflies. Females of this species are often streaked with blue.

Yuk! Looks like a squishy bird dropping! In fact, it is the glossy larva or caterpillar of the Orange (Citrus) swallowtail butterfly.

Even the beetle's head is bright red, adding to the warning-color effect.

Several flowers mimic insects, such as this Cretan bee orchid. Bees visit it with the aim of mating, and carry away its pollen instead.

Bright and conspicuous warning colors, as in this Red lily beetle, are a vital part of mimicry. Red is a danger signal in nature – a fact which this beetle uses to its advantage. We respond to the color red in the same way, hence danger signs often have red backgrounds.

❑ Mimicry is very common among butterflies. In the U.S.A., the Viceroy butterfly impersonates the bad-tasting Monarch. In Florida, where Monarchs are rare, the Viceroy mimics the Jamaican danaus butterfly.

❑ In Africa, there are more than 100 different colorations of females in the butterfly species known as the Mocker swallowtail. Each kind is a mimic of a different species of distasteful butterfly. The male butterflies, however, have no problem choosing females of their own species. They can spot the difference.

❑ In fact, there are two main kinds of mimicry, both named after famous naturalists. These are called Mullerian mimicry, after H.J. Muller, and Batesian mimicry, after W.H. Bates. Both naturalists studied and collected insects in South America. In Mullerian mimicry, animals of different kinds, which are all distasteful or harmful, have very similar warning colors. A predator who encounters one of them is then more likely to leave alone any similar-colored animal. In this way, all the mimics gain. In Batesian mimicry, a harmless animal pretends to be a harmful or distasteful one by its colors, patterns, shape, or even its smells and sounds. The harmful animal it copies is called the model. The mimic gains protection, the model gains nothing.

Courtship – take your partners!

The vast majority of female animals must mate with a male of their own kind, before they can produce young. Sometimes a female and male come together by chance, mate quickly, and go their separate ways. But in other cases the animals, like people, have a 'courtship.' They send signals to one another, by sights, sounds, smells, tastes, and touches, before mating. There are examples in most animal groups, from worms to apes. The male stickleback fish swims a zig-zag dance, waves his fins and shows off his red belly to the female. The female Two-lined salamander will not mate until the male bites her back! One of the most elaborate performances is by the male Blue bird of paradise. He shimmers his amazing plumage, sings an incredible song, and even hangs upside down on the branch – all to impress the female. Courtship has several purposes. It ensures that animals only mate with others of their own species, who send and receive the correct signals in the correct sequence. This avoids making mistakes with other, similar species! It helps to ensure that both partners are mature and in breeding condition. If one is not ready, she or he does not carry on the display. And when several animals – usually males – display together, it helps the female to choose the strongest, finest male to be the father of her offspring.

The extraordinary courting display of the male Emperor bird of paradise involves a loud squawk, then upside-down shimmerings of his beautiful blue plumage.

Male spiders carefully court the larger, more poisonous females. The orb-web male (on the left) strokes the female as she eats a fly he has presented to her, to assess if she is yet ready to mate.

❏ The male praying mantis must be extra-careful as he courts the female. He creeps up from behind and jumps on to her back. Otherwise, if she could grab him, she would eat him alive!

❏ Dungflies carry out their rapid courtship in a very odd place – on a cowpat or other pile of droppings, where the female will lay her eggs!

In the breeding season, dozens of frog species croak to attract mates. The Gray treefrog picks out its own species' call from the general clamor.

The purpose of courtship is to mate and produce young. Here a year-old tiger cub nuzzles its mother for a meal. She will feed it on milk for another six months or so. During this time she ignores or repels the advances of courting males in the vicinity. Only when the cub is weaned, will she be ready to mate again.

In this time-lapse photograph, male fireflies trace out tiny streaks of greenish light, as they flash courting signals to the females nearby.

❏ Some animals flash light signals to their mates as part of their courtship. Fireflies (which are really beetles) and lanternfish do this.

❏ The old saying 'mad as a march hare' refers to courtship. In spring, male and female hares race about, leap and chase each other, and even rear up and 'box' with their front paws. This looks like crazy behavior to us, but it is part of the hares' courting ritual, as they show each other how healthy and agile they are.

Breeding – getting the chemistry right

In nature, sexual reproduction is the main method of producing young. Genes are the microscopic molecules that contain all the instructions for building and running a living thing. In sexual reproduction, genes from the female's egg and the male's sperm mix together at fertilization, to produce a new combination of genes in each offspring. It means that each youngster is slightly different from its parents, and also slightly different from its brothers and sisters. This variation gives each individual a unique chance of survival in nature's struggle for existence. Variation is the 'raw material' for natural selection to work on, in the process of evolution. At the level of genes, the process is the same for all living things. But the ways in which animals and plants form breeding groups, and how much effort they put into raising young, vary enormously. The same female and male Golden eagles stay together for many years. They have few young, and look after them well. By contrast, sea urchins simply cast their eggs and sperm into the sea water, and leave fertilization and the survival of the young to chance. Many flowers have both male and female parts, but they avoid fertilizing themselves by a variety of means. If they did self-fertilize, their offspring would lack the vital genetic variation.

Male and female swans swim 'cheek to cheek,' part of their pair-bonding behavior which keeps them together as a couple for many years.

The male European toad may cling to the back of his partner for several days, until she lays her eggs. Then he sheds sperm to fertilize them.

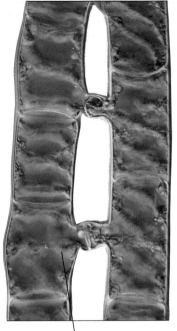

Some plants 'mate,' too. These hair-sized filaments of a simple plant, the alga *Spirogyra*, are transferring cellular material. This process is called conjugation.

An unmistakable portrait: the male mandrill, largest of the monkeys. His facial coloring is repeated at his rear end. The colors may serve to excite the females at breeding time. Many male monkeys mate with several females.

❑ When a tigress is in heat (ready to mate) her urine and feces take on a special smell that attracts males. The males fight with one another to win over the tigress but usually do not harm one another. Mating takes only a few seconds. The tigress may mate with more than one male.

❑ In biology, one female mating with one male is known as monogamy. If a male mates with several females, or a female mates with several males, this is called polygamy.

❑ One of the most 'faithful' birds is the albatross. Some pairs have stayed together for more than 30 years.

❑ A hermaphrodite animal has both male and female sexual parts. Snails are hermaphrodites, but they cannot 'mate with themselves.' A snail mates with another snail (as seen above), and each fertilizes the other.

Protecting eggs – slime, shells, and guardians

Animals and plants have evolved all manner of ingenious ways of protecting and looking after their eggs and seeds, as the young develop inside. In plants, the eggs are protected inside the receptacle as the flower shrivels and the seeds form. Animal eggs left to hatch on their own, without the parent guarding them, usually have a protective outer coating. This can be leathery, as in the egg-cases of whelks (a type of sea snail), fish such as sharks and rays, and reptiles. Or it may be slimy and slippery, as are the jelly-covered spawn of frogs, toads, newts and salamanders, water snails, and some rockpool fish. Many insects hide their tiny eggs in cracks and crevices, often in a place where the young can easily find food. The woodwasp drills into a tree with her spear-like ovipositor (egg-laying tube) and lays the eggs in the solid wood. When the larvae hatch, they eat the wood! Some animals carry their eggs with them, including certain spiders and scorpions, insects like cockroaches, and some worms and frogs. Birds usually stay with their eggs, since they must be kept warm or the developing young inside will die. Most birds sit on the eggs in a nest and use their own body heat as the source of warmth, a process known as incubation.

Lesser-spotted dogfishes develop in leathery egg cases. After hatching, empty cases may wash up on the beach as 'mermaid's purses.'

Instead of a nest, Australia's Mallee fowl parents make a yard-high mound of rotting vegetation. The eggs incubate in the warmth within.

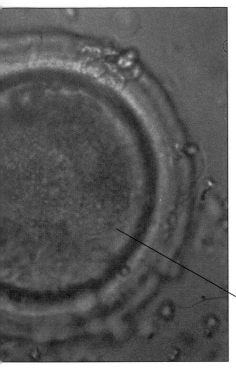

The slimy, slippery covering of frog spawn is difficult for a predator to penetrate. It also protects the developing tadpoles from frost.

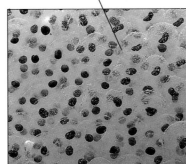

This microscope photograph shows a human egg cell in the fallopian tube. In real life it is one two-hundredth of an inch (0.1 mm) across.

Birds keep eggs warm, but not hot. The Magellanic penguin lets the breeze cool its shaded egg, to prevent overheating and premature hatching.

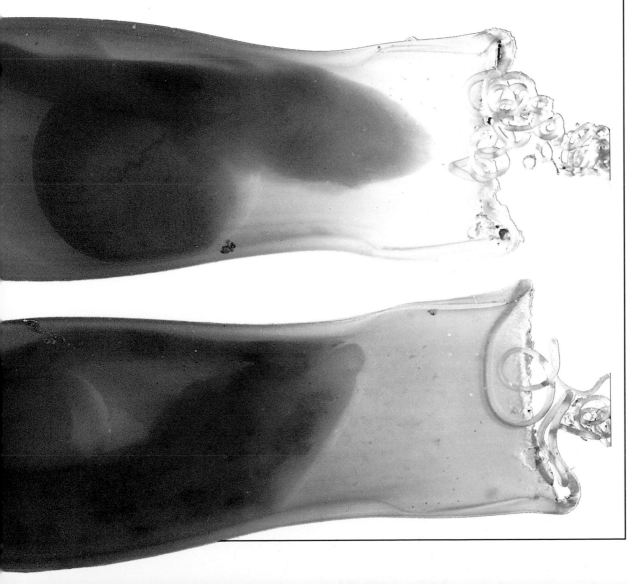

Parental care – looking after baby

While caring for her baby, the mother langur keeps an extra-careful watch for possible dangers and threats around her.

Baby animals that are born or hatch, and then have to fend for themselves, are statistically unlikely to survive. To make sure enough of them grow up to carry on the species, the female has to produce many offspring – sometimes even millions. At the other end of the spectrum are animal parents that have very few offspring, but who put much time and effort into caring for them. Among the insects, the wasps, bees, ants, and termites make large nests where the developing young are fed, protected, and cared for. Among fish, the mouthbrooding cichlids let their fry (baby fish) swim to the safety of their mouth when danger looms. Among reptiles, the mother crocodile guards her young in a quiet 'nursery creek' part of the river. Birds and mammals show the most complicated parental behavior, as they gather food for the offspring, clean the nest, and keep the young free of parasites. Indeed, the young of most mammals develop safely within their mother's body, and are fed on milk for a time after birth – a special form of parental care. The instincts (built-in reactions) of parents when they are protecting and defending their young are some of the strongest in nature. Few animals of any kind are as dangerous as a mother and/or father guarding their young.

A baby langur monkey clings to its mother. The mother feeds the baby on milk, cleans it, and protects it. This takes time and energy, but the baby has a good start in life, and the mother is sure it will survive.

76

In most human societies, parents care for their offspring in a family group longer than any other animal parents.

A female wolf spider carries her offspring on her back. The baby spiders cannot open their tough egg sacs by themselves, and rely on her to do so.

In marsupial mammals like Bennett's wallaby, the mother carries her young in a pouch. Over the weeks the youngster grows rapidly from a thumb-sized baby, and spends more time outside the pouch.

A Gray whale calf spends its first months close to its mother. She will protect it from enemies like Killer whales. Like all baby mammals, it feeds on her milk for a period after birth.

❑ The female scorpion is an attentive mother. She gives birth to her young over a period of weeks, one or two at a time. The young ride on her back for a week or two, well protected by the poisonous sting just above!

❑ Baby mice who crawl out of the nest and get lost make ultrasonic squeaks, too high-pitched for us to hear. The mother hears them, finds the babies, and returns them to the nest.

❑ A Sperm whale mother feeds her calf on more than 45lb (22kg) of fat-rich milk – every day! The youngster will continue to suckle for a little over 12 months.

Instinct and learning – doing what comes naturally?

A parrot that says 'Who's a pretty boy?', or a similar phrase, has no real understanding of the meaning. It simply mimics sounds.

A newborn baby can do very little except sleep, suck milk, and cry! But it can perform some actions straight after birth. If you stroke its cheek, it turns its head to that side. This is called the rooting instinct, and it helps the baby's mouth to find the milk. A year later, the same baby has learned to smile, say a few simple words, crawl, and perhaps even walk. These two basic types of behavior, instinct and learning, occur in differing proportions throughout the animal kingdom. An instinct is present from birth and the animal can perform a function without being taught or copying another. A snail that feels a knock on its shell draws itself inside, and a deer fawn that senses danger lies still in the undergrowth. These types of behavior patterns are somehow built into the animal's genes. Learned behavior comes from experience, trial and error, and copying and imitation. The animal tries an action, and remembers the result. Successful behavior is repeated in similar situations. Learning and memory may involve new or changing connections between the animal's nerve cells – especially in its brain. The brain is constantly 'rewired' to reinforce successful actions, and discourage unsuccessful ones.

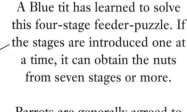

A Blue tit has learned to solve this four-stage feeder-puzzle. If the stages are introduced one at a time, it can obtain the nuts from seven stages or more.

Parrots are generally agreed to be among the most intelligent birds. They can distinguish shapes, colors, and even small numbers. Many learn to perform tricks for a human audience, like walking a tightrope.

Are car-assembly robots clever? They carry out repetitive tasks such as welding accurately. But they do nothing until programed by their human masters. They can, of course, be taught new tricks by changing the programs.

The single-celled organism *Paramecium,* lacking brain or nerves, has simple built-in behavior patterns. It swims away from too-bright light or poisonous chemicals.

Animals like these sealions are taught circus tricks like this by conditioning – making them do it many times until a signal from the trainer sets off the action automatically.

❏ Even animals as 'simple' as beetles and sowbugs can learn. In an experimental maze, after several tries, they are quicker at taking the correct route to get to the food.

❏ Some birds can 'count.' They are shown a sign with a certain number of dots, then a selection of containers with different numbers of dots. They peck at the container with the same number of dots as the sign – it contains food.

❏ Acorn woodpeckers of North America drill short holes in tree trunks and wedge acorns into them as food stores for the winter. They fiercely defend these larders against other woodpeckers and hungry squirrels and jays. A single tree may hold up to 50,000 stored acorns!

❏ Memory is not the same as learning, but it is an important part of learning. Studying people, scientists have recognized several types of memory. Short-term memory is used, for example, when you look up a number in the phone book. You remember the number long enough to dial it, then a few minutes later, it has gone! Medium-term memory lasts for days or a few weeks. You may use it to remember an appointment at the dentist. Weeks later – the memory has gone. Long-term memory lasts for years. You use it mainly for important and significant things, such as your home telephone number.

Living alone – benefits and pitfalls

Humans are social animals. A few people are 'loners,' but most of us live in groups and like the company of others. We learn from one another, and share ideas and information. Most of our close animal relatives, the apes and monkeys, are also group-dwellers. But many other creatures, from tigers to tarantulas, live a solitary life. They only come together with others of their kind for a short time, to mate and/or raise young. Living alone has certain advantages. A single creature has a good chance of hiding or escaping from a predator. The predator can detect a large group more easily, by sight and by the increased noises and smells that the group makes. A lone hunter is also able to sneak up on prey more effectively, especially in the undergrowth. Living alone means the animal does not have to compete directly with others of its kind, if food or water is scarce. Often, a solitary animal sets up its own territory, which supplies it with food, and which it defends against neighbors of its own species. Some night-active animals are solitary, partly because it is difficult for them to stay together in a group in the dark!

Unhindered by nearby trees, this lime may reach 130ft (40m) in height when full-grown, after about a century.

Trees growing on their own, such as this lime, can reach their full size and natural branching pattern. In a close group, they compete for light and their shape is altered.

Small, simple creatures such as this pond *Hydra* are not able to interact and have a social life. If they gather together at one place, it is only because conditions are suitable there.

In the Asian vegetation, the tiger's stealthy stalk-and-charge hunting methods are part of its solitary way of life. Only 1 in 20 attacks are successful.

The tarsier of Southeast Asia hunts alone at night. But a male and female usually share the same territory.

A herd of African elephants is usually led by an older female, the matriarch. Adult males generally live alone or in small bachelor groups.

❏ Of the big cats, only lions live in groups. The tiger, leopard, cheetah, jaguar, Snow leopard, and Clouded leopard are all solitary hunters.

❏ The Water chevrotain, a type of small deer, is one of the most solitary members of the deer group. If a male meets a male, he may bite with his small but sharp tusks (canine teeth) for a few seconds. If a male meets a female, they mate for about 5 minutes. Otherwise, Water chevrotains have nothing to do with one another.

❏ Living alone in the immense depths of the sea could mean problems in finding a mate. When the female deep-sea anglerfish finds a male, he attaches to her body, and lives on her like a parasite. He is always available for breeding!

❏ Some holly trees never bear berries – because they are male! Even some female trees rarely have berries. This is because there are no male trees nearby to supply the pollen, which is needed to fertilize the flowers and make them ripen into berries.

❏ Some animals are simply too dangerous to live together. Most sharks are solitary because they eat anything – including members of their own species! They only gather in groups where there is plentiful food to be had.

Living in groups – the community spirit

'Safety in numbers' is one advantage of living in groups. A huge herd of zebras or wildebeest has hundreds of pairs of eyes, ears, and nostrils alert and ready to sense danger. Once the warning is given, the herd scatters and a predator may find it difficult to pick out one victim from the mass of bodies. Fish such as cod, herring, mackerel, and tuna live in great shoals that twist and turn in unison. To a predator, the shape of the whole shoal may look like one very large animal, and again it is difficult to single out one victim. There are advantages in feeding, too, since many eyes, ears, and nostrils search for food. As a flock of starlings pecks in a field, the members watch one another. If one finds a rich supply of food, the others gather round, to get their share. In group-living predators, several animals may cooperate to catch one large victim that provides plenty of food for all. Living in groups may also help at breeding time. In a gull colony, there are so many eggs and chicks that predators are 'swamped.' They cannot eat them all.

Zebras and wildebeest mingle on the African plains. An alarm from one sets off the vast herds on an escape run.

The alligator's mottled coloring merges perfectly with bankside stones and plants. Camouflage is important for a predator.

Barracudas sometimes swim in dense shoals like this, especially when prey is plentiful. At other times they split up and hunt singly.

This Thomson's gazelle stands alert on the edge of the herd. It is on the lookout, as the others feed quietly behind.

Puffins rest in huge groups. A predator might snatch one, but the others have an excellent chance of escape.

Although they are deadly and powerful hunters, alligators are surprisingly tolerant toward one another. They gather in groups to bask and feed peacefully together. The females lay their eggs and bring up their young communally.

FACT FILE

❏ In contrast to the big cats, most members of the dog family - wolves, hunting dogs, jackals, hyenas – live and hunt in groups. Within a wolf pack, there is a dominant male and female that mate together for life. Subordinate males and females will fight among themselves and challenge to be leaders of the pack. If they fail, they are usually driven out. Or they may leave the original pack and try to set up packs of their own. When hunting, though, all adults work together as a team to track down and ambush prey.

❏ The most common fishes are bristlemouths, which form huge shoals and live in all oceans. They are usually less than 2in (5cm) long, and are caught in tens of thousands by trawl nets.

❏ Locusts form the biggest groups of animals, known as swarms. These cover up to 95 sq miles (250km^2) and may contain tens of millions of individuals. But locusts are not truly social animals in that there is no division of labor within the swarm. The insects do not interact and respond to each other.

❏ Living in a group means you have to eat your share of food quickly, before others get it. The dhole, or Asian wild dog, can gulp down 9lb (4kg) of meat in less than one hour. This is equivalent to an adult human eating 40lb (18kg) of meat at one meal!

Pecking orders–showing them who's boss

Living in a social group presents a problem. If a dispute breaks out, perhaps over food or a mate, what stops the rivals fighting about it? Constant disorder would endanger the survival of the members. Who keeps the peace? In most social groups there is a natural order, or dominance hierarchy. One dominant animal is the 'chief' and in charge. If he or she is involved in a dispute, the challenger usually backs off. The subdominant animals are next in line, and so on, down to the ordinary members of the group. These types of societies occur in several animal groups, such as insects and birds. But they are most common among mammals, and especially among the primates (lemurs, bushbabies, monkeys, and apes). In an elephant herd, a senior female is in charge; in most baboon troops, it is a male. The dominant animals usually have the best food, mates, and resting places. Occasionally the chief animal is challenged by a younger, stronger individual. This is part of natural selection. It makes sure that the most able and powerful individual becomes dominant. In a gorilla troop, the dominant male or 'silverback' beats his chest, roars, and thrashes the branches, to frighten off a leopard or a rival male.

A well-trained army has a dominance hierarchy, which we call a ranking system. Badges and stripes on the uniform show the rank.

Grooming is an important part of the baboon hierarchy. A subordinate animal always grooms a dominant one first, then is groomed in return.

The pecking order of chickens in the farmyard determines who gets the best roosts and who mates with the rooster.

In this gorilla troop the large old male, or silverback, positions himself between his family and the photographer so as to protect them.

Kangaroos and wallabies 'box' to establish their positions in the hierarchy. These males are sparring to attract a female mate.

FACT FILE

❏ The hierarchy-type social system was noticed among farmyard chickens. The dominant ones were rarely pecked by the others, but pecked them often. The lowest members were pecked by all the others, but could not peck back. This is why such systems are called 'pecking orders!'

❏ Within a group of gorillas, the dominant male does not keep his position by being the strongest but just by being the oldest (and therefore the largest). Females squabble among themselves by barking, screaming, grappling, and biting one another, but when it comes to mating, they each accept the advances of any adult male.

❏ In Rhesus monkeys, high-ranking females give birth to more daughters than sons, while low-ranking females have more sons than daughters. How this happens is not known.

Altruism – helping others to help yourself

This Alpine marmot is ready to warn others in its family of danger. Even if attacked, it will have helped some of its genes to continue – those carried by the family members, especially its offspring, who made it safely back to the burrow.

Life has been described as a struggle for existence. The purpose of any animal or plant is to survive. But in nature, some animals deliberately help others of their kind, while putting themselves at risk. In an extreme example, why should a worker honey bee sting an intruder in the hive, when this means her certain death? This behavior is called altruism: when one animal helps another, but gets nothing in return. It may even suffer or be killed. The reasons why altruistic behavior comes about involve genes. In evolution, the purpose is to survive *and* have offspring – in other words, to contribute as many genes as possible to the next generation. A mother animal defends her offspring to the death, because half of their genes came from her (the other half was from the father). Helping the offspring to survive helps her genes to carry on, and is better than them all being killed. The worker bee is doing the opposite, in that she helps to defend her mother, the queen, who has some of her genes. Close relatives such as sisters, aunts and uncles, and cousins, also have genes in common. So altruistic behavior also involves helping members of one's family. It is better that a few of one's genes live on than none at all. In this way, it seems that genes themselves may direct an individual's action. This has led to the 'selfish gene' idea. Darwin's original theory of evolution concerned the struggle for survival among whole animals and plants, but the modern concept is based on competition among genes. Even among genes, life means 'survival of the fittest.'

The members of this elephant herd are closely related and have many genes in common. They all help to carry on a shared 'gene pool.'

Lionesses pounce on a doomed African buffalo. The members of the pride are relatives, and they share genes – and the meat of the victim.

Older brothers and sisters in a Green woodpecker family show altruistic behavior, cooperatively helping to feed the nestlings.

❑ The reasons that cause animals to display altruistic behavior were first explained in terms of genes by William Hamilton, in the 1960s. The way this behavior evolves is known as kin selection – helping your kin (relatives), so as to help some of your own genes to pass on to the next generation.

❑ In an elephant herd, the adults are a mixture of mothers, daughters, and sisters. They live as a family group and all help to protect and raise the babies. This way, they all help to pass on a group or 'pool' of genes. Male elephants stay separate and often wander around together in groups. Occasionally they have shows of strength with one another, with the victor going off in search of females with which to mate.

❑ Flocks of Green woodhoopoes of East Africa number up to 20 birds but contain only one pair of breeding birds. Juvenile birds help their parents to feed nestlings.

❑ Ants in a nest show altruistic behavior when they attack a predator such as an anteater. They all join in the battle and put themselves at risk not knowing which of them will survive. By contrast, Slave-maker ants are tyrants not altruists. They catch members of other ant species and make them into 'slaves' to care for their own young.

Division of labor – from jack-of-all-trades to the ultimate specialist

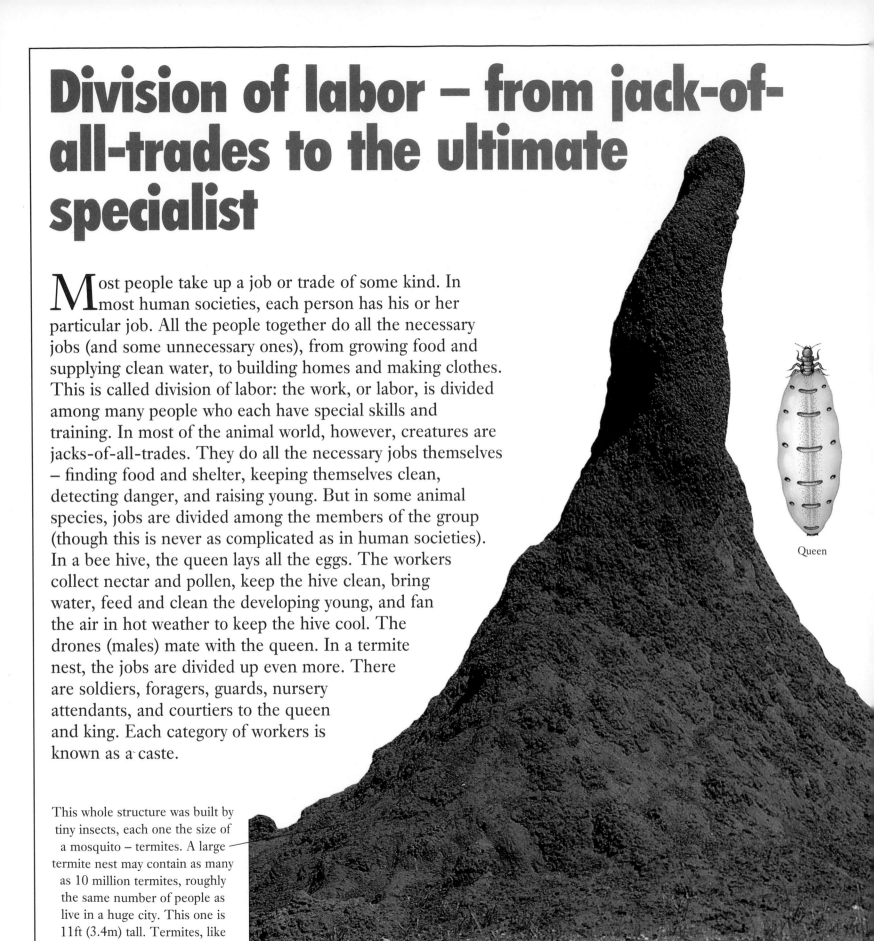

Most people take up a job or trade of some kind. In most human societies, each person has his or her particular job. All the people together do all the necessary jobs (and some unnecessary ones), from growing food and supplying clean water, to building homes and making clothes. This is called division of labor: the work, or labor, is divided among many people who each have special skills and training. In most of the animal world, however, creatures are jacks-of-all-trades. They do all the necessary jobs themselves – finding food and shelter, keeping themselves clean, detecting danger, and raising young. But in some animal species, jobs are divided among the members of the group (though this is never as complicated as in human societies). In a bee hive, the queen lays all the eggs. The workers collect nectar and pollen, keep the hive clean, bring water, feed and clean the developing young, and fan the air in hot weather to keep the hive cool. The drones (males) mate with the queen. In a termite nest, the jobs are divided up even more. There are soldiers, foragers, guards, nursery attendants, and courtiers to the queen and king. Each category of workers is known as a caste.

Queen

This whole structure was built by tiny insects, each one the size of a mosquito – termites. A large termite nest may contain as many as 10 million termites, roughly the same number of people as live in a huge city. This one is 11ft (3.4m) tall. Termites, like bees, practice division of labor.

Naked mole rats from Africa are the only mammals which form insect-like colonies. The 'queen rat' is the only female who breeds.

King   Soldier   Worker

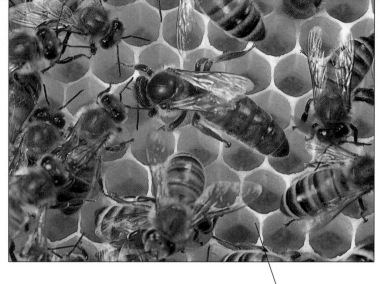

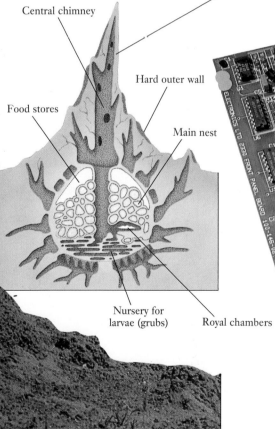

Central chimney

Hard outer wall

Food stores

Main nest

Nursery for larvae (grubs)

Royal chambers

A cut-away view of a termite mound, showing the main nest below ground level, and close-ups of the main types or castes of termites.

A queen bee inspects the six-sided comb cells before laying her eggs in them. Workers look after all the needs of this · egg-laying machine.

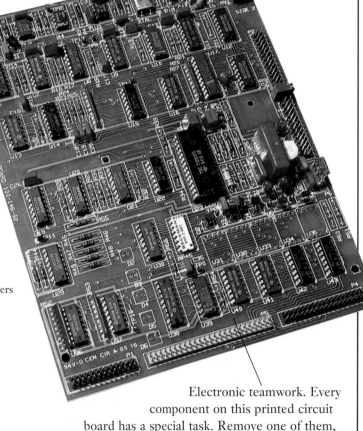

Electronic teamwork. Every component on this printed circuit board has a special task. Remove one of them, and the board no longer functions. The components are said to be integrated.

Tools – using, making, designing, and inventing

Some time ago, tool-using was considered one of the main characteristics that separated humans from animals. Our inventiveness, ingenuity, and clever hands have come up with a vast array of tools, from prehistoric stone axes and wooden spears, to wrenches, electric drills, and computers. Then naturalists watching animals in the wild discovered that many of them also used tools, mostly in a simple but still effective way. Chimps poke a grass stem or twig into a termite nest so that the termites crawl on to it, then they pull out the twig and lick off the juicy termites. Several birds use tools. The Woodpecker finch of the Galapagos Islands pokes insects out of bark crevices with a thin twig or cactus spine. The familiar thrush smashes snail shells open on a flat stone, its 'anvil,' to get at the tasty snail flesh inside. There were so many examples that tool-using was no longer seen as a distinctively human ability. Some experts suggested that making a tool, rather than just using something that was lying around, was unique to humans. But chimps break the twiglets off a twig to make their ant- or termite-poker. They tear and crush leaves into a 'sponge' to mop up water in a crack or hole, which they cannot reach otherwise. Probably, many other examples of tool-making and tool-using are waiting to be discovered in the animal world.

Masai people make a small wound in one of their cattle to let out some blood, for use as food and in traditional ceremonies. A hunting tool – the bow and arrow – makes the slight wound.

Floating on its back, a Sea otter puts a flat pebble on its chest, and smashes shellfish on it to get at the flesh.

This chimpanzee prods the water with a simple tool, a stick, in an attempt to dislodge an object below. Chimps are noted for their use of tools.

❑ The earliest known human tools are 2.5 million years old, from northeast and east Africa. They are blocks of lava and other rocks, crudely chipped to make rough hand-axes and choppers. Their makers were probably the earliest humans, creatures called *Homo habilis*, who may have been our ancestors. The name *Homo habilis* means 'handy man,' referring to his tool-making abilities.

❑ The next type of human, *Homo erectus*, made more finely-shaped stone tools such as scrapers, chisels, knives, and choppers. These are from about 1.5 million to 300,000 years old.

❑ The Neanderthal people lived in Europe and the Middle East during the Ice Ages, from about 150,000 to 35,000 years ago. They made stone tools, including spear-heads and ax-heads.

❑ The Egyptian vulture often picks up stones in its beak and throws them at ostrich eggs to break them open in order to feed on the contents.

Snails (this is a Banded snail) are soon broken open on the thrush's tool, a stone anvil. Several types of birds use stone tools like this to get at their food.

The Archer fish spits a stream of 'water bullets' at an insect on a leaf or twig above the water. The insect falls in, and the fish gobbles it up.

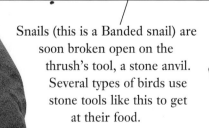

Play – waste of time, or training for life?

As young Squirrel monkeys play, they learn important skills for their tree-top life. They find out how to grip the branches securely and keep their balance.

Young horses rear and buck as if jumping for joy. One day these actions will be serious, as they compete against herd members for dominance and mates.

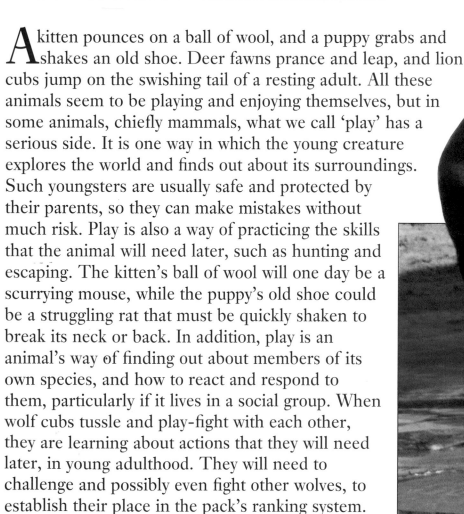

A kitten pounces on a ball of wool, and a puppy grabs and shakes an old shoe. Deer fawns prance and leap, and lion cubs jump on the swishing tail of a resting adult. All these animals seem to be playing and enjoying themselves, but in some animals, chiefly mammals, what we call 'play' has a serious side. It is one way in which the young creature explores the world and finds out about its surroundings. Such youngsters are usually safe and protected by their parents, so they can make mistakes without much risk. Play is also a way of practicing the skills that the animal will need later, such as hunting and escaping. The kitten's ball of wool will one day be a scurrying mouse, while the puppy's old shoe could be a struggling rat that must be quickly shaken to break its neck or back. In addition, play is an animal's way of finding out about members of its own species, and how to react and respond to them, particularly if it lives in a social group. When wolf cubs tussle and play-fight with each other, they are learning about actions that they will need later, in young adulthood. They will need to challenge and possibly even fight other wolves, to establish their place in the pack's ranking system.

❏ Most play can be seen as training for later life. But there are many examples where scientists cannot agree that playing is helpful in this way. Could it be that the animals are really just enjoying themselves, and having fun?

❏ Adult whales and dolphins sometimes leap from the water and crash back again on their sides. This is called breaching, and some experts say it may be a type of play. Another suggestion is that it helps to remove parasites clinging to their skin.

❏ One strange type of play is seen when young otters slide down a riverbank mudslip into the water. Even adults may join in. It is hard to see how this may be useful in later life. Possibly it is a quick way of reaching the safety of the water when being chased by a predator.

❏ Antelope seem to play by leaping almost straight up, stiff-legged, and 'bouncing' along. This is called stotting or pronking. But research has shown that predators do not often chase antelopes that stott well. The stotting may be a way for antelopes to show predators how healthy and agile they are. The predator chooses an antelope that stotts less well, and which would be easier to catch.

As kittens pounce on each other, they hone the hunting techniques on which their wild ancestors depended.

Elephant calves wallow and wrestle in the muddy water. They also spray water over one another with their trunks. In later life, strength and pushing power will help them to overcome rivals and gain mates for breeding – their ultimate aim in life.

Intelligence – how do we define it?

Through the ages, in many cultures, people have argued about the meaning of the term 'intelligence.' Is it a general ability to remember, recall, learn, and solve problems? The intelligence tests used by certain schools and organizations have changed over the years, and there are several versions in use today. Some experts say these tests are helpful as a general guide. Others say that no single test could measure general intelligence in all humans. People vary so much in their experiences, and what is seen as important and a sign of intelligence in their own culture. There are similar problems when we try to apply the word 'intelligence' to other animals. How similar is it to learning? Creatures such as squirrels and tits can learn to make their way along a complicated feeder, pulling levers and pressing bars in the correct sequence, until they get food as a reward. But this seems to be more trial-and-error learning, than true intelligence. One aspect of intelligence is the ability to consider and solve a problem not by trial and error, but by thinking about it first. The solution is worked out mentally (in the brain), perhaps as a result of what we call inspiration or insight. Only a very few creatures, such as gorillas and chimps, can think and solve problems in this way.

Birds vary markedly in their intelligence. A sparrow could not do this parrot's 'trick.'

In nature, these two mammals are predator and prey. Yet the Killer whale has been trained to eat the fish, not the Galapagos sea lion.

Octopuses are among the most intelligent invertebrates. Their behavior is very varied and adaptable.

This zoo gorilla has realized that scooping water with its hand creates currents, that bring bits of food thrown into its moat by visitors.

The sea lion has learned to suppress its natural escape behavior, in return for a reward of a fish meal. Life in captivity is not all bad.

❏ Intelligence is not vital for success in the natural world. One of the most successful animals in terms of numbers is the housefly, yet we would not regard it as a particularly clever creature!

❏ Intelligence is not necessarily connected with brain size. Some animals have much bigger brains than us, such as whales and elephants. Yet we would not regard them as cleverer than us. An average human brain weighs 46 ounces (1,315g), while a whale's brain weighs four times as much.

❏ IQ means Intelligence Quotient. A person scores marks on one of the IQ-type tests, such as the Stanford-Binet test. The score is compared with the person's real age in years to give the IQ.

❏ Intelligence may be related to the size of the brain compared to the size of the body – the body:brain ratio. In an elephant this is 650:1, in a dolphin 125:1, and in a human about 40:1.

❏ Brain size and intelligence was no real guide to evolutionary success in the past. The dinosaur *Stegosaurus* had a huge body weighing 1.5 tons, and a tiny brain the size of a hen's egg. Its body:brain ratio would have been about 15,000:1. Yet these dinosaurs survived for tens of millions of years.

Adapting and evolving – keep up, or die out

The idea of evolution is central to a scientific view of the natural world. Evolution simply means change with time. Animals and plants change, or evolve. Evidence for this comes from fossils, the remains of living things that died thousands and millions of years ago. Older fossils are different from the fossils of recent times. But why do living things evolve? In general, and in the wild, life is a competition to find food, or water, or a space to live, or light (for a plant). Any feature that gives a living thing an advantage over others will help it to survive and produce offspring. A plant that grows faster can get more light and out-shade its neighbors. An animal with bigger claws can catch prey more easily. If this feature is passed to the offspring, they will have a better chance of survival, too. They are better fitted, or adapted, to their surroundings. It is as though nature is selecting which ones will die and which will live – the process of natural selection. As animals and plants breed, variations and new features appear. The environment changes too, as the climate becomes hotter or colder over thousands of years. So evolution is a continual process, as living things change to win the struggle for life, and develop new adaptations to the changing environment.

People have selected and bred many varieties of flowers, such as the Canterbury bellflower. This process is called artificial selection.

This chick hatched from an egg laid in the host nest by the cuckoo's mother. Cuckoos may lay up to 25 eggs in the course of a season.

Blue tits have learned to peck at bottle tops to get at the delicious cream. It is a small example of how behavior evolves.

The urge to feed its offspring makes this dunnock care for a nest imposter, the huge cuckoo chick. The cuckoo has adapted as a brood parasite. It cannot survive any other way.

In the past two centuries, Red foxes have adapted their hunting behavior. Now they scavenge for 'easy pickings' in towns and cities.

Fossils – this is a trilobite – show that living things in the past were different from those today. Trilobites died out 220 million years ago. They were related to modern crabs and insects.

The Pacific islands of Hawaii formed over five million years ago, from underwater volcanoes. It is thought that a few honeycreepers flew there from mainland America, and evolved into different species, with beaks suited to different foods in different ecological niches. The shape of each beak is related to the food which it must eat.

Iiwi

Apapane

Food: nectar, insects

Kauai akialoa

Maui parrotbill

Akiapolauu

Food: insects

Ou

Food:fruit

Grosbeak finch

Food: seeds

Ancestral honeycreeper

❑ The dinosaurs ruled the land for 150 million years. Yet they could not evolve to survive some unknown change in the world, and they died out quite quickly about 65 million years ago.

❑ Herring gulls normally eat anything they can find, including scraps of food on garbage heaps. But among a group of Herring gulls on Walney Island, Cumbria, England, some individuals feed mainly on mussels, others upon earthworms, some on rock crabs, and a fourth group on the eggs and chicks of other gulls. Competition has forced them to become specialist feeders.

❑ The stable-fly bites warm-blooded creatures, such as cattle and people, to feed on blood. It can withstand air temperatures ranging from 57-89°F (14-32°C). The house-fly feeds on all sorts of decaying material. Its temperature tolerance is from 68-104°F (20-40°C). Each species has become adapted for quite different ways of life.

❑ Extinction is a natural process. Over 99 percent of all animal and plant species that have ever lived on Earth are now extinct. The problem is that human activities, such as pollution, hunting, and destroying wild places, have greatly speeded up the rate of extinction.

Dying – the end of the road, but life goes on

No living thing lasts for ever. A single germ such as a bacterium has a 'life' of only 15-20 minutes, until it divides into two new germs. Some types of fly hatch from their eggs, feed and grow as maggots, change into adult flies, and lay their own eggs – all in less than three weeks. Many small plants and creatures, such as weeds, worms, and insects, live for only one year. Bigger animals and plants take longer to grow, so they live for several years. Toward the ends of their lives, plants and animals are more likely to become diseased, or weak, or injured, and they fall victim to predators more easily. In nature, an animal or plant is usually killed, rather than dying of old age. Humans are an exception. In most human societies, older people are cared for. There are several theories of ageing, which try to explain why living things grow old. The microscopic cells that make up the body are always dividing, to replace cells that wear out or die. It may be that mistakes in cell division gradually happen more often, and eventually the cells cannot do their jobs. Or a vital organ such as the heart can only beat so many times, before it wears out and stops supplying the body with blood. This is like a vital part in a machine wearing out, such as the engine in an automobile. Whatever the reason, living things are born, grow up, breed – and then die.

Life in the slow lane: a Galapagos giant tortoise does not rush. Continued growth through life means that large reptiles, such as turtles, snakes, and crocodiles, are very old.

Machines, like living things, have a finite lifespan. Most modern cars 'die' after ten or fifteen years. Unfortunately, and unlike living things, they do not rot away easily, back into the soil. But parts of them can be recycled.

Signs of ageing in the human body include skin wrinkles and graying hair. But the brain may stay very active. Many human societies value the experience and wisdom that age confers on the elderly.

Some Californian Giant sequoias are over 4,000 years old. It takes this long to accumulate such a huge bulk, often about 260ft (80m) high and 80ft (24m) in circumference.

This disease-causing *Staphylococcus* bacterium has lived its life in minutes – killed by an antibiotic drug that upset its internal chemistry.

❏ Some of the 'tallest tales' about people, animals, and plants have been about the great ages they could achieve. The bible story of Methuselah, which says he lived to the age of 969 years, cannot be supported by modern science.

❏ Humans are among the longest-lived mammals. In a country such as the U.S.A. or U.K., the average age at death is more than 70 years. Some elephants and whales have lived to this age, but in the wild their average age at death is much lower.

❏ The oldest humans for whom there are proper records have rarely lived beyond 110 years. The oldest person of modern times may be a Japanese man, Shigechiyo Izumi, who died in 1986, aged 120 years. It seems that women stand a greater chance of reaching 100 than men. Nearly four in five living centenarians are female.

❏ Some of the longest-lived organisms are creosote plants and bristlecone pine trees of western North America. They are more than 5,000 years old.

❏ The longest-lived animal may be the quahog, a clam-like shellfish. Some individuals are said to be more than 200 years old.

❏ The oldest giant tortoise lived to about 150 years of age. The oldest bird, a Sulfur-crested cockatoo, was over 80.

SUPERFACTS

SUPERFACTS

Great in number

There are probably more than 30 million different types of living creature. In the animal world, there are more insects than all kinds of other animals put together – upwards of 1 million species. Mollusks – slugs, snails, limpets, mussels, squid, and octopuses – are the second most common type of animal, and protozoans the third. However, bacteria make up more than 75 percent of all living things. ▶

Long-jumper

Fleas can jump up to 200 times their own length. This is equivalent to a person jumping a distance of nearly a quarter of a mile (400m). ▼

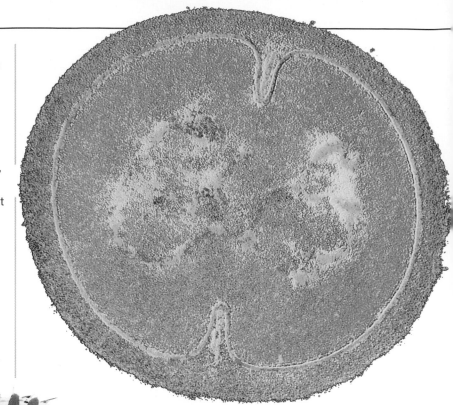

Bright sparks

Electric eels store enough electricity in their tails to light up 12 household light bulbs.

Big eaters ▼

A snake may take a year to eat its own weight in food. An elephant may achieve this feat in a month, a seabird in a day, and a tiny shrew in about 5 hours. We take about five weeks to do this. We each eat an average of 1,000lb (450kg) of food a year. An Indian python can eat a 120-lb (54.5-kg) leopard in one go but then it does not need to eat for days.

The fastest movers

On land, the fastest creature is the cheetah. It can reach speeds of over 60mph (96km/h). Antelope can sprint at 60mph (96km/h). We can manage only 23mph (37km/h). In the air, the Spine-tailed swift can fly at over 106mph (170km/h), although a Peregrine falcon can, in a dive, reach speeds of over 200mph (320km/h). The sailfish is the fastest creature in water, reaching more than 60mph (96km/h), and possibly nearly 70mph (113km/h).

The most offspring

The Ocean sunfish lays as many as 300 million eggs, and the edible mussel up to 25 million. Various crustaceans – crabs, lobsters, and shrimps – also produce more than 1 million eggs. A queen termite may lay 30,000 eggs a day for several months. The African elephant produces just one offspring at a time, as humans usually do. About 1 in 80 human births are twins, and 1 in 6,500 are triplets.

The greatest traveler

The Arctic tern migrates every year from the Arctic to the Antarctic and back, a round-trip of 22,000 miles (35,400km). A swift that died aged 21 years old probably covered nearly half a million miles (750,000km) in its lifetime, migrating to and from southern Africa and Europe each year.

Incubation periods

The Brown-headed cowbird of North America lays its eggs in other birds' nests, and they hatch after an incubation period of only about 10 days. In this way, the young cowbirds hatch before the foster-parents' eggs, which they often throw out of the nest. The Wandering albatross has the longest incubation period of any bird, at up to 85 days.

The most poisonous

Chemicals secreted by the skin of some poison-dart frogs of South America are the deadliest of natural poisons. They can kill a person in less than a minute. The venoms of cobra and viper snakes are less powerful, yet more people die from snake bites – some 30,000 each year. The venom of a Black widow spider can kill a child, and a sting from various African and North American scorpions can kill an adult in about 45 minutes. Death cap is the world's most poisonous fungus. The leaves of foxgloves and all parts of the Deadly nightshade and laburnum plants are poisonous to people.

Population size

The number of people in the world today probably exceeds 5,000 million. Insects such as aphids, locusts, and ants are considerably more numerous. A single swarm of locusts can contain several trillion individuals. And there are more living organisms on the skin of a single human than there are people on the Earth. ▼

Eyeballing

Whales have fixed eyeballs and have to move their whole body to see in a different direction. Owls can turn their heads fully round half a circle so have all-round vision. Chameleons have eyes on turrets that can swivel round independently. They can look in two directions at once.

The call of the wild

The call of the Humpback whale is the loudest noise made by a living creature. At 150 decibels, it is almost as loud as Concorde taking off. Sounds travel faster and farther in water than on land, and it is believed that humpbacks can hear one another over distances of more than 200 miles (320km).

Skyscraper

Termite colonies build spiral mud towers up to 20ft (6m) tall – the height of a large motor coach. Within them they construct ventilation and cooling ducts and chambers in which they cultivate fungi. The tall towers are built principally to cool the underground chambers.

SUPERFACTS

Beating wings

When threatened, a midge can increase the speed of its wingbeats to more than 2,000 beats per second. Hummingbirds can beat their wings at more than 80 times a second. ▶

Born to fly

The Sooty tern can fly for up to four years without landing. It feeds and sleeps on the wing and lands only to mate and lay eggs.

High-flyers

On their migrations, storks fly at altitudes of 16,000ft (4,875m) and geese at up to 28,000ft (8,535m) – about the height of Mount Everest. Jet aircraft fly at about 35,000ft (10,660m) although Concorde goes up to 50,000ft (15,250m) or more when flying supersonic.

The oldest animal ▶

The longest-lived animal for which there are accurate records is a tortoise from the Seychelles. It is more than 155 years old. Among mammals, humans have the longest lifespan. The average lifespan in developed countries is between 70 to 76 years, but there are accurate records for tens of thousands of people alive today who are more than 100 years old. There are also records of an elephant that lived for 81 years and a cow that was at least 78 years old when it died in 1975.

Long sleep ◀

We sleep an average of 7½ hours a day. However, some people have managed to stay awake for over 400 hours. The Barrow ground squirrel of North America hibernates underground for longer than any other creature – 9 months of the year – but during this period it occasionally wakes and feeds. The Two-toed sloth sleeps up to 20 hours a day, and a cat about 13 hours. Horses, elephants, cattle, and deer can sleep standing up. The swift sleeps on the wing.

The most children

In the 18th century, a Russian peasant woman reportedly gave birth to 69 children. In recent times, Maria Olivera of Argentina has given birth to 32 children.

Role reversal

Among the Spotted sandpipers of North America, the females are the dominant sex. Each adult female will have several male mating partners. She is larger than the males, and will fight with other females to attract and win over males. Having laid her eggs, she then leaves the male to incubate the eggs.

Food for all ▶

Garbage heaps provide food for cats, dogs, foxes, rats, raccoons, jackals, bears, and birds. In this way, many wild animals have got used to living in towns. In Florida, a heap of household rubbish about the size of a football field attracted a flock of more than 14,000 birds to it, where they scavenged for food.

Animal mathematicians

Clever Hans was a horse that apparently could count. When its master called out a number, the horse would tap the same number of times on the ground with its hoof. However, it was shown that Hans was clever not at counting but at sensing small subconscious actions of his anxious master that indicated when he had achieved his task – a raising of the eyebrows or a sigh of relief.

Animal talkers ▷

A chimpanzee, Washoe, learned a vocabulary of more than 150 signs and used them in small combinations to make herself understood to her trainers. Another female chimp, Lana, was taught to operate a computer keyboard with colored symbols in order to 'talk' to her trainers. She could tell them she wanted a drink or something to eat.

Imprinting

Austrian animal behaviorist Konrad Lorenz showed that newborn ducks, geese, sheep, and cattle will latch on to the first thing they see and follow it around as if it were their mother. Young Greylag geese imprinted on Lorenz used to walk behind him in a line as if following their mother. Similarly, a mother goose, denied contact with her young when they hatch, will not be imprinted with their smell and will reject them.

Territories

One of the largest of territories held by an animal is that of hunter-gatherer people such as the Bushmen, or San, of the Kalahari Desert in Africa. A group of 20 will have a territory of about 270 sq miles (700km^2). A tiger's territory is about 50 sq miles (130km^2), and a Golden eagle's about 27 sq miles (70km^2). One of the smallest is that of the Sage grouse of America. It is a circle about 35ft (11m) in diameter.

Survival of the species

It is estimated that there are more than 30 million species of plants and animals on Earth today. But as we build over, pollute, or destroy their living space, we are wiping them out at at the rate of 18,000 each year. About 200,000 more species will vanish by the year 2000.

SUPERFACTS

Deadlier than the male

The malaria parasite *Plasmodium* has caused more human deaths than any other creature. Each year it claims the lives of several million people in the tropics, and there are at least 400 million cases of malaria worldwide. The microscopic creature is spread by the female *Anopheles* mosquito as it feeds on human blood.

Squirmy wormies

Worms are the largest parasites of the human body. The pork tapeworm that lives in the intestines can grow to 30ft (9m) in length. The World Health Organization (WHO) believes that a quarter of the world's population are infected by the roundworm *Ascaris*.

Teeming with life ▶

The tropical rainforests of South America and Southeast Asia comprise the richest plant and animal communities on Earth. More than a third of all the trees in the world grow in these forests. The marine equivalent of these wildlife reserves are the coral reefs of Australia and the West Indies. The Great Barrier Reef off eastern Australia is the home to more than 3,000 different species of invertebrate (animal without a backbone), ranging from jellyfish and sea anemones, to crabs, starfish, and sea slugs.

White sea slugs (above), coral reef fish (right), and a rain-forest hot lips plant (below) – part of nature's amazing profusion.

Eat and be eaten

More than 90 percent of all sea creatures end their lives being swallowed by other animals. Zooplankton – the tiny animals that float or swim in surface waters of seas and oceans – are food to all sorts of shellfish, fish, and to the baleen whales such as the Blue whale, the largest creature on Earth. Many of these animals are in turn eaten by others, which eventually may fall victim to the largest predators, among them sharks and Giant squid.

All puffed up

Puffer fish inflate their spiny bodies with water when disturbed to avoid attacks by predators but the Japanese puffer has an added deterrent. It carries a poison more deadly than curare, the plant chemical South American Indians use to tip their poison arrows. This can kill a person within a few hours.

Color change ▼

Just as chameleons can change their skin color to blend in with their surroundings, so can some species of fish. Flatfish are masters at this, being able to change the color and distribution of pigments in their skin to match almost any seabed. Fusilier fish living around coral reefs change color to camouflage themselves as the amount of sunlight penetrating surface waters varies during the day. In the mornings they take on a pale bluey color and at night, when they sleep on the reef, they become reddish underneath and dark gray on top.

Helping one another

Among deep-sea angler fish, the females of some species are more than 20,000 times larger than the males. The males spend their adult lives as parasites on the females, getting all their food from them. In return, the males fertilize the females' eggs as soon as they are laid.

Blowing hot and cold

During the day in the desert, when air temperatures can exceed 110°F (43.3°C), a camel's body may heat up to 105°F (40°C). At night, when air temperatures can drop below freezing (32°F/0°C), it may fall to 93°F (33.9°C). A camel has little fat in its skin – most of it is stored in its hump – so heat readily escapes from it body. At night, its woolly fur retains much of its heat. Like many desert animals, it has a light-colored skin. This reflects lots of sunlight during daytime, and helps prevent overheating. ▶

Mountain zones

Plantlife on a high mountain reflects, according to its altitude, definite zones similar to those found when traveling from the equator to the north pole. At the bottom there is deciduous forest, then coniferous forest, alpine vegetation, tundra, and finally polar vegetation. Near the summit of Mt. Everest, at 29,028ft (8,848m) the world's highest peak, there are seeds and pollen deposited by the wind, and – even at this altitude – on these feed insects and their relatives, among them beetles, millipedes, mites, and springtails.

King of the beasts ▲

The lion is often regarded as the most dangerous animal. It will even prey on elephants, which are many times larger, and on crocodiles, which most other animals leave well alone. (However, an adult elephant can fend off a lion, and in the water a crocodile will overcome one.) People – with the invention of the gun, far more deadly than any wild animal – also prey on crocodiles, mostly illegally to obtain their skins to make handbags, shoes, and wallets. Mankind is probably the deadliest animal on the globe.

INDEX

Page numbers in **bold** indicate major references including accompanying photographs. Page numbers in *italics* indicate captions to illustrations. Other entries are in normal type.

The American grizzly bear is one of the largest of all living land carnivores. Though it is certainly a fierce predator, much of its food consists of grasses, fruit, and berries.

PICTURE CREDITS

The publishers wish to thank the following photographers and agencies
who have supplied photographs for this book. The photographs have
been credited by page number and position on the page: (B) Bottom,
(T) Top, (C) Center, (BL) Bottom Left, etc.

Boeing Aerospace: 56-57(T)

Eric and David Hosking: 8 (G.E. Hyde),
23(TR), 24-25, 26-27, 37(BL), 40(C),
47(C), 49(C), 50(T), 52(BC), 56(TL),
64-65, 70-71, 76, 78(R), 81(T), 84, 85(T),
85(C), 96-97, 100-101, 101(CL), 102(B),
103(BL)

Frank Lane Picture Agency:
R. Austing: 13(B), 34(T), 55(BR), 81(C),
89(TL)
B. Borrell: 38(BL)
Hans-Dieter Brandl: 20(B), 73(B), 86,
87(TR), 94(T)
W. Broadhurst: 13(T)
B.B. Casals: 16
P. Davey: 83(T), 84-85, 86-87, 87(TL)
T. Davidson: 89(TR)
Norman Duerden: 91(C)
Eichhorn-Zingel: 105(BR)
FLPA/Frank Lane: 52(BL), 55(T), 59(TR),
91(B), 95, 98-99
Tom and Pam Gardner: 74
A.R. Hamblin: 83(C)
Frants Hartmann: 19(B), 58-59, 90-91(B),
92-93(B)
H. Hautala: 66-67
Peggy Heard: 72(T)
Roger Hosking: 45(T)
W. Howes: 33(B)
R.P. Lawrence: 10(T), 10-11, 59(TL),
77(BL), 85(B), 97(TR)
M.D. Mackay: 70(T)
S. Maslowski: 36-37, 62(B)
G.J.H. Moon: 47(B)
Mark Newman: 29(T), 29(C), 54, 59(C),
103(BR)
Philip Perry: 55(C), 66(C)
Fritz Pölking: Title page, 19(T)
K.G. Preston-Mafham/Premaphotos Wildlife:
23(TC), 35(BL), 49(T), 68(BL), 68(TR),
70(B)
A.A. Riley: 82
D.A. Robinson: 13(C)
Leonard Lee Rue: 11(TR), 42, 49(B), 61(C),
90-91(T)
S. Schrempp: 65(TR)

Julie Swale: 43(C)
M.J. Thomas: 80-81
R. Thompson: 96
Roger Tidman: 27(B), 58
R. Van Nostrand: 75(TR)
Maurice Walker: 18(BL)
J. Watkins: 39(B)
B.M. Wellman: 77(BR)
Larry West: 48(T), 71(T)
Anthony Wharton: 29(B), 48-49, 67, 75(TL)
Terry Whittaker: 18-19, 48(B), 60-61(B)
R. Wilmshurst: 15(B), 60-61(T)
D.P. Wilson: 74-75(B), 94(B)
W. Wisniewski: 41, 45(B), 72(B), 88-89,
103(TL), 106
M.B. Withers: 15(TR), 27(C), 28(B), 40-41,
78(L)
J. Zimmermann: 51(T), 79(B)

Ministry of Defence, London: 40(B)

Science Photo Library:
Sally Bensusen: 55(BL)
Biophoto Associates: 15(TC)
Martin Bond: 17(C)
Dr. Jeremy Burgess: 12, 17(B), 46(T)
Oscar Burriel/Latin Stock: 82-83(B)
Jean-Loup Charmet: 44(B)
Andy Clarke: 27(T)
CNRI: 24(BL), 99(C), 100(T)
Darwin Dale: 34(BL)
Martin Dohrn/Stephen Winkworth: 37(T)
Vaughan Fleming: 51(CR), 66(B), 69(T)
Eric Grave: 79(C), 80
David Hardy: 38-39
Adam Hart-Davis: 16-17
John Howard: 36(B)
Bruce Iverson: 25(B)
Keith Kent: 71(C)
Mehau Kulyk: 24(BR)
John Mead: 28-29, 99(T)
Peter Menzel: 11(TL), 42-43(T), 56(B), back
endpaper
Astrid and Hanns-Frieder Michler: 62(T)
Novosti: 15(TL)
Claude Nuridsany and Marie Perennou: Half-
title page, 20(T), 26(BL), 30(BC), 30-31(C),
31(B), 42-43(B), 66(TL), 101(B), 105(BL)

David Parker: 44-45
Petit Format/Nestle: 74-75(T)
Philippe Plailly: 47(T)
Dr. Morley Read: 33(T), 33(C), 50(B), 52-53,
61(T), 63(B), 68(BR), 104(BL)
John Reader: 12-13
Roger Ressmeyer, Starlight: 35(BR)
Shirley Richards: 32
Peter Ryan, Scripps: 17(C)
Robin Scagell: 46-47
David Scharf: 10(B), 100(B)
Heini Schneebeli: 57(T)
Andy Snow: 79(T)
SPL: 38(BR)
Sinclair Stammers: Front endpaper, 50-51,
97(C)
Sheila Terry: 89(B)
Dr. T.E. Thompson: 104(T)
Cath Wadforth: 25(T)
M.I. Walker: 73(T)

Silvestris/Frank Lane Picture Agency:
A.N.T.: 53(T)
Daniel Bohler: 97(TL)
Dani/J. Jeske: 18(T), 56-57(B)
Devez: 62-63
Siegfried Kerscher: 77(TR)
Erhard Kotzke: 69(B)
Karin Krone: 65(TL)
Eva Lindenburger: 93(TR)
Anton Luhr: 102(T)
Robert Maier: 92
Stefan Meyers: 105(TR)
Müller: 31(T), 77(TL)
Dietmar Nill: 35(T)
Jörg Reimann: 98(B)
Ingo Riepl: 22-23, 82-83(T), 104(BR)
Walter Rohdich: 23(B)
Norbert Rosing: 30-31(B)
Sea World: 14-15
Silvestris: 21(TR), 32-33, 72-73, 81(B),
91(TR), 92-93(T), 94-95
Otto Stadler: 98(T)
Sunset: 20-21
Klaus Uhlenhut: 63(T)
Maximilian Weinzierl: 53(B)
Konrad Wothe: 37(BR), 61(B), 65(B)

Monarch butterflies migrate annually from Canada to Florida to overwinter there.